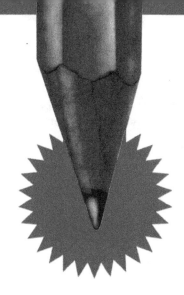

GRAMMARWORK

4

English Exercises
in Context

PAMELA PETERSON BREYER

Longman

Aquisitions Editor: Mary Jane Peluso
Management of Development Services: Louisa B. Hellegers
Development Editor: Carol Callahan and Penny La Porte

Director of Production: Aliza Greenblatt
Editorial Production/Design Manager: Dominick Mosco

Manufacturing Manager: Ray Keating
Production Supervision/Electronic Page Composition: M.E. Aslett Corporation
Art Director: Merle Krumper
Cover Design: Marianne Frasco
Electronic Art: Warren Fischbach
Interior Design: Patrice Fodero
Interior Art: Lane Gregory and Dorothea Sierra

© 1996 by Prentice Hall Regents

Pearson Education
10 Bank Street
White Plains, NY 10606

Printed in the United States of America
25 26 27 28 29 30 V092 16 15

ISBN 0-13-340274-6

Printed on Recycled Paper

To my cousin Becky Greene Myer

CONTENTS

Conditionals

Modals and Idiomatic Modals

Clauses

Pronouns

INTRODUCTION

Recent studies have shown that students acquire and retain a new language more rapidly and more efficiently when the structure and vocabulary of the language are presented in context; that is, when elements of a lesson, such as grammar and new lexicon, are tied together in some real and meaningful setting. Exercises that present material in such a situational context are referred to as contextualized exercises.

GrammarWork is a series of four contextualized exercise books for students of written English. These books may be used as major texts or as supplementary material, depending on whether a course is nonintensive or intensive. Each exercise in each book presents, as a unit, vocabulary relating to a particular context and structures that are appropriate to that context.

Book One is intended for the beginner: the student enrolled in a first-level English course who has had some exposure to the language. Book Two continues with beginners' material, proceeding from first-level to second-level work. Book Three is designed for the intermediate student, and Book Four contains material appropriate to high-intermediate levels.

The books are organized into grammatical units (i.e., the Verb *To Be*, Present Continuous, Simple Present). Each unit contains a variety of exercises with practice in small increments. Most units include more than one exercise on key grammar points, in order to give students sufficient and varied practice. Also included in each unit are review exercises and periodic tense contrast exercises, usually located at the end of the unit.

The pages in each book are, for the most part, divided into three sections:

a. an examination of the structure to be presented (**Grammar**);

b. exercises that enable the student to manipulate that new structure in a contextual setting (**Practice**); and

c. a culminating exercise activity in which the student uses the material in the exercise by applying it to some personal, real-life situation (**Make It Work**).

The **Grammar** section shows the student how to use the structure to be practiced, with diagrams and arrows that should be self-explanatory. Notes of explanation are supplied only when the grammar rule cannot be illustrated sufficiently.

The **Practice** section consists of a contextualized exercise, usually a page in length and always self-contained; if a context is three pages instead of one, it will be self-contained within those three pages. Thus the teacher can select any exercise or group of exercises he or she considers appropriate for a particular class, lesson, or given time. The teacher can choose to utilize all the exercises in the order presented. The exercises have been arranged in ascending order of difficulty, with structures generally considered to be the easiest for most students presented first.

The exercises are self-contained in that they have been designed for written practice without necessarily being preceded by an introductory teacher's presentation. Since grammatical diagrams have been included and the new vocabulary is usually illustrated or defined, students can work independently, either at home or in class—in pairs or as a group. When students work together in pairs or in groups in the classroom, they should be encouraged to help each other; the teacher, too, can assist by circulating from pair to pair or group to group, guiding and correcting.

The **Make It Work** section enables students to apply what they have been practicing to freer, and sometimes more natural, situations. The activity usually contains a picture cue, a fill-in dialogue, or questions to answer. The purpose of the **Make It Work** section is to provide the student with as real-life a setting as possible.

The perforated answer key can be used by either the student or the teacher. The teacher may choose to withhold the answers on some occasions; on other occasions, the students may use the answer key for self-correction.

IT'S ON A WOODED LOT WITH TREES ALL AROUND IT.

-s vs. No -s with Countable Nouns

Simple Present

singular	plural	
a tree	trees	many trees
one tree	two trees	all of the trees
	several trees	

Note: For words ending in a consonant + *y*, drop the *y* and add *ies*.
berry → berries   baby → babies   lady → ladies

PRACTICE

Fill in the blanks with the singular or plural form of the noun.

Bruce: My wife and I just bought a new _____*house*_____ .
                                                                    (1. house)

Chuck: What's it like?

Bruce: It's on a wooded _____ with _____ all around it.
                                          (2. lot)   (3. tree)

Chuck: Is it one _____ or two?
                              (4. story)

Bruce: Two _____ . It has four _____ on the first floor
                    (5. story)   (6. room)

and three on the second floor.

Chuck: Is it in good condition?

Bruce: Yes, but several _____ need to be painted.
                                    (7. room)

Chuck: Well, that's easy to do. Is the kitchen modern?

Bruce: Yes. It has a _____ , and all of the _____ are new.
                              (8. dishwasher)   (9. cabinet)

Chuck: How many _____ does it have?
                              (10. bathroom)

Bruce: Two and a half. It has a half _____ downstairs and two
                                                    (11. bathroom)
_____ upstairs.
(12. bathroom)

Chuck: It sounds great. Good luck in your new house.

BASEBALL AND BIOGRAPHIES

Countable and Uncountable Nouns

countable nouns	uncountable nouns	
games	fields of study:	English, engineering
biographies	actions or states:	living, gardening
	sports:	golf

Note: Add *s* to countable nouns. Don't add *s* to uncountable nouns. Fields of study, actions or states, and sports are usually uncountable nouns.

PRACTICE

Bargain Book Company offers readers a large selection of books about the subjects listed below.

Make the countable nouns plural.

1. architecture _____ —
2. art _____
3. baseball _____
4. biography _____
5. chemistry _____
6. cooking _____
7. dictionary _____
8. engineering _____
9. English _____
10. fishing _____
11. game _____
12. gardening _____
13. health _____
14. hobby _____
15. Japanese _____
16. music _____
17. mystery _____
18. pet _____
19. photography _____
20. tennis _____

MAKE IT WORK

Name two categories you're interested in.

travel _____

_____

_____

New Word: biography = the story of a person's life

I'D LIKE MORE FRIENDS. I'D LIKE FEWER ACQUAINTANCES.

Noun Comparisons with *More, Less,* and *Fewer*

> I'd like more friends.   I'd like fewer acquaintances.
>
> I'd like more fun.   I'd like less work.
>
> Note: Use *more* with countable and uncountable nouns.
>   Use *fewer* with countable nouns; use *less* with uncountable nouns.
>
>   Abstract words, emotions, and general classes are usually
>   uncountable.

PRACTICE

Tell if you would like *more, less,* or *fewer* of the following things in your life. Fill in the blanks.

1. I'd like _____*more*_____ fun.

2. I'd like _____*less*_____ work.

3. I'd like _____ time to myself.

4. I'd like _____ love.

5. I'd like _____ problems.

6. I'd like _____ happiness.

7. I'd like _____ sadness.

8. I'd like _____ arguments.

9. I'd like _____ money.

10. I'd like _____ stress.

11. I'd like _____ encouragement.

12. I'd like _____ criticism.

13. I'd like _____ friends.

14. I'd like _____ acquaintances.

MAKE IT WORK

Name one thing you would like more of. _____

Name one thing you would like less of. _____

New Words: stress = mental or emotional strain or tension
        encouragement = giving hope or courage to someone
          criticism = giving an unfavorable opinion

NEW CITY HAS THE FEWEST SCHOOLS OF THE THREE.

	New City	Midland	Bridgetown
Population	1,867,760	1,453,343	1,652,794
Schools	201	311	284
Firefighters	1,846	762	1,287
Police Officers	3,935	2,503	3,125
Criminal Offenses	218,571	50,649	111,935

Note: When *crime* is a general category, it is uncountable. When it is an individual act, it is countable.

NEW CITY HAS THE FEWEST SCHOOLS OF THE THREE.

Noun Comparisons with *Less, The Least, Fewer,* and *The Fewest*

Simple Present

New City has	fewer	schools than Bridgetown.
New City has	the fewest	schools of the three cities.
Midland has	less	crime than Bridgetown.
Midland has	the least	crime of the three.

Note: Use *fewer* and *the fewest* with countable nouns. Use *less* and *the least* with uncountable nouns. *More* and *the most* are used with both countable and uncountable nouns.

PRACTICE

Look at the chart on page 4. Then compare the three cities. Fill in the blanks with *less, fewer, the least, the fewest,* or *the most.*

1. Bridgetown has _____ *fewer* _____ people than New City.

2. New City has _____ *the most* _____ people of the three cities.

3. New City has _____ schools of the three.

4. Midland has _____ schools of the three.

5. Midland has _____ firefighters of the three.

6. Bridgetown has _____ firefighters than New City.

7. New City has _____ firefighters of the three.

8. Midland has _____ police officers of the three.

9. Bridgetown has _____ police officers than Midland.

10. Bridgetown has _____ police officers than New City.

11. Midland has _____ crime than Bridgetown.

12. By far, Midland has _____ crime of the three.

13. Bridgetown has _____ crime than New City.

14. New City has _____ crime of the three.

15. And yet, New City has _____ police officers of the three.

MAKE IT WORK

Name one reason to live in Midland.

_____

AMERICANS LOVE HAMBURGERS.

Review: Countable and Uncountable Nouns

Simple Present

uncountable nouns	countable nouns
(general category)	(specific item)
clothing	a shirt, hats
food	a hamburger, apples
information	a report
engineering	an engineer, doctors

Note: Sports, abstract nouns, and general categories are usually uncountable.

PRACTICE

Fill in the blanks with the singular or plural form of the noun in parentheses.

According to the latest _____*information*_____ in *Facts* Magazine,
　　　　　　　　　　　　　　　(1. information)
America's favorite pastime is watching television. A recent

_____ says that the average American watches TV about
　　　(2. report)

four _____ a day. America's favorite sports activities are
　　　　　(3. hour)

_____ and _____ . Seventy million
　　　(4. walking)　　　　　　　　(5. swimming)

people walk, and sixty-six million people swim regularly.

_____ is the number one outdoor pastime.
　　　(6. gardening)

The average American earns $24,670 a year. _____
　　　　　　　　　　　　　　　　　　　　　　　　　(7. miner)

and _____ have the most stressful jobs, although they are
　　　(8. police officer)

paid less _____ for their _____
　　　　　(9. money)　　　　　　　　　　　　(10. work)

than other occupations. _____ have the least
　　　　　　　　　　　　　　　(11. librarian)

_____ on the job.
　　　(12. stress)

What's America's favorite drink? _____ , of course.
　　　　　　　　　　　　　　　　　　(13. coffee)

AMERICANS LOVE HAMBURGERS.

Americans drink seventeen million _____ of it a day. Their
(14. gallon)

favorite snack is _____ . The average American eats
(15. ice cream)

sixteen _____ of it a year. Americans also love
(16. pound)

_____ . The average American eats a _____
(17. hamburger)   (18. hamburger)

three times a week. Americans spend millions of _____
(19. dollar)

on their pets. Sixty-two million Americans own _____ ,
(20. cat)

and fifty-three million people own _____ .
(21. dog)

Can you guess what article of _____ Americans wear
(22. clothing)

most often? _____ . College _____
(23. blue jean)   (24. student)

wear them one-third of the time.

MAKE IT WORK

Answer the questions.

What's your favorite pastime?   _____

What's your favorite sport?   _____

What's your favorite drink?   _____

What's your favorite snack?   _____

What's your favorite article of

clothing?   _____

New Word: pastime = something that helps to pass the time

IS THERE AN EMPLOYMENT AGENCY IN THIS AREA?

A vs. *An*

a	delicatessen	an	attorney
a	furniture store	an	exterminator
a	restaurant	an	inexpensive restaurant
		an	optician
a	university, but	an	unusual gift shop
a	hobby shop, but	an	honest insurance agent
		an	X-ray technician

Note: Use *an* before words that begin with vowel sounds; use *a* before all other sounds.

PRACTICE

Fill in the blanks with *a* or *an*.

1. ___*a*___ hairdresser
2. ___*an*___ attorney
3. _____ plumber
4. _____ licensed electrician
5. _____ insurance agent
6. _____ automobile mechanic
7. _____ reliable babysitter
8. _____ honest tax accountant
9. _____ optician
10. _____ dentist
11. _____ experienced painter
12. _____ dependable gardener
13. _____ exterminator

14. _____ locksmith
15. _____ good dry cleaner
16. _____ hospital
17. _____ X-ray laboratory
18. _____ animal hospital
19. _____ university
20. _____ employment agency
21. _____ unusual gift shop
22. _____ inexpensive restaurant
23. _____ hardware store
24. _____ appliance center
25. _____ health food store

MAKE IT WORK

Ask two questions about stores and services in your area.

Is there an employment agency in this area?

_____

_____

New Words: locksmith = a person who makes and repairs locks

exterminator = a person who kills unwanted animals and insects

8

ICE CREAM MELTS. AN ICE CUBE MELTS.

No Article vs. A and An

Name something that melts.

	ice cream
a	snowman
an	ice cube

Note: Use *a* or *an* with singular countable nouns.
Don't use *a* or *an* with uncountable nouns.

PRACTICE

Give two answers for each statement. Write only singular words.

Name two things that melt.

1. *ice cream* _____

2. _____

Name two things you polish.

3. _____

4. _____

Name two things you button.

5. _____

6. _____

Name two things you tie.

7. _____

8. _____

Name two things you eat by the slice.

9. _____

10. _____

Name two things that are delivered every day.

11. _____

12. _____

Name two fruits you can eat without peeling.

13. _____

14. _____

Name two things you buy by the gallon.

15. _____

16. _____

MAKE IT WORK

Compare your answers with a classmate's.

New Word: peel = remove the outer covering

SHE GOT A SUITCASE FROM THE BEDROOM CLOSET.

A vs. *The*

Simple Past

> She looked up at the sky. The sun wasn't shining.
>
> She took an umbrella and left the house.
>
> Note: Use *the* when you refer to only one of something: the sky   the sun
>
> Use *the* for things at home or in the community when people know which one you are talking about: the car   the windows
>
> Use *a* or *an* for unspecified objects: an umbrella   a sweater
>
> Do not use *a* or *an* with plural or uncountable nouns: clothes   weather

PRACTICE

Fill in the blanks with *a* or *the*.

1. She got ___*a*___ suitcase from ___*the*___ bedroom closet.

2. Then she put _____ pair of jeans and _____ T-shirt into the suitcase.

3. She also packed _____ nightgown and _____ sweater.

4. She went into _____ bathroom and looked into _____ medicine cabinet.

5. She took _____ toothbrush and _____ comb.

6. Then she walked downstairs and watered _____ plants.

7. She closed _____ windows and pulled down _____ shades.

8. She locked _____ door and left _____ house.

9. As she got into _____ car, she noticed _____ clouds in _____ sky.

10. She hoped _____ sun would come out.

11. She hoped that _____ weather would be good.

12. She got into _____ car and drove to _____ airport.

MAKE IT WORK

Answer the questions.

Where do you keep your suitcase?

_____

Where do you keep your umbrella?

_____

SHIRTS WERE HALF-PRICE. I BOUGHT A SHIRT.

No Article vs. *A* or *The*

Simple Present, Present Continuous, Simple Past, Future with *Will*

[ ] Shirts were half-price.

I bought [a] shirt for my husband. [The] shirt cost $10.00.

I bought two shirts for my husband. [The] shirts I bought were $10.00 each.

Note: Do not use an article for general statements.

Use *a* and *an* for a single unspecified object, especially when mentioning it for the first time.

Use *the* for a particular object, especially when it is followed by a modifier or when it has been mentioned before.

PRACTICE

Fill in the blanks with *a* (or *an*), *the*, or a line for no article (—).

1. Smith's Farm Market is ___an___ outdoor market.

2. It sells everything from _____ antiques to fresh vegetables.

3. _____ market opens at 7:00 on Tuesday and stays open all day.

4. But you have to be there early if you want to get _____ parking space.

5. By about 8:00, Smith's Market is packed with _____ people.

6. If you are looking for _____ vegetables, you'll find top quality and unbeatable prices.

7. Last week, for instance, I bought _____ entire basket of tomatoes for only 89¢.

8. _____ mushrooms I bought were only $1.00 a pound.

9. You'll also get good buys on _____ household goods like _____ mops and _____ brooms or even _____ sheets and _____ towels.

10. I bought _____ sheet and _____ two towels for the total price of $16.00.

11. _____ sheet was $8.00, and _____ towels were $4.00 each.

12. At any department store, _____ sheets sell for about $16.00 each.

13. You can also buy _____ clothes at Smith's Market.

14. I bought _____ beautiful wool sweater there.

15. _____ sweater cost $13.95.

16. There were items like _____ watches for sale.

17. _____ watches they were selling were name brands like Timex and Bulova.

18. I bought _____ watch for only $9.00.

19. I also saw _____ rug for $20.00. Now I'm sorry I didn't buy it.

20. Next week I'm going back to Smith's Market, and if _____ rug I saw is still there, I'll buy it.

MAKE IT WORK

Tell about the last time you went to a sale.

I went to a fantastic sale at _____ . _____
_____ on sale. I bought _____
_____ . _____ cost only
_____ . I also _____
_____
_____

HE'LL GO TO SCHOOL IN THE FALL.

No Article vs. *The* with Expressions of Time and Place
Simple Present, Simple Past, Future with *Will*

expressions with *the*	expressions without *the*
the beginning, the end	at [ ] first
the past, the present	at [ ] noon
in the evening	[ ] January 23rd
in the fall	go to [ ] school, college
the 23rd of January	go to [ ] church
go to the university	go [ ] home
go to the bookstore	

PRACTICE

Fill in the blanks with *the* or a line for no article (—).

1. Kosho plans to go to _____ college _____ next year.

2. He'll go to _____ school in _____ fall.

3. The first semester begins on _____ September 15th and lasts until _____ middle of January.

4. The second semester begins at _____ end of January and continues until _____ 20th of May.

5. At _____ first, Kosho will be very busy getting used to his new schedule.

6. His courses begin at 8:00 in _____ morning and last until _____ noon.

7. After he goes to _____ cafeteria and eats a quick lunch, he'll go to _____ work.

8. He has a part-time job in _____ afternoon.

9. At _____ night, he'll go _____ home and study.

10. He's worried about _____ future. He doesn't know if he can handle a job and his schoolwork.

MAKE IT WORK

Tell about your English course.

It started in _____ . It began on _____

and lasts until _____ . It meets on _____

at _____ in _____ .

	place names without *the*	place names with *the*
continents, states, cities	North America, Texas, Philadelphia	
countries	Canada	the United States
points of the compass	northern New York	the North

bodies of water
  rivers, oceans
 	
  lakes, bays
	
	Lake Ontario, Hudson Bay
		
		the East River
		the Atlantic Ocean

mountains
  mountain ranges
 	
  single mountains
	
	Mt. Fuji
		
		the Catskill Mountains
		(the Catskills)

islands
  single islands
  a group of islands
	
	Liberty Island
	Hawaii
		
		the West Indies

hotels	Madison Hotel	the Hilton Hotel
museums, libraries		the Metropolitan Museum the New York Public Library
streets	Forty-second Street	the Avenue of the Americas
colleges, universities	New York University	the City University of New York
bridges		the Golden Gate Bridge
parks, squares	Central Park Times Square	
beaches	Waikiki Beach	

Note: Use *the* if a proper noun is plural: the United Nations, the West Indies.
Use *the* with proper nouns that contain *of* phrases: the Statue of Liberty.

A TRIP TO THE METROPOLITAN MUSEUM AND CENTRAL PARK

No Article vs. *The* with Place Names

NEW YORK!
Now only $2,690!

PRACTICE

Look at page 14. Then fill in the
blanks with *the* or a line for no article (—).

1. ▶ two weeks in ___the___ United States

2. ▶ round-trip airfare from _____ South America to _____ New York

3. ▶ a room with a private bath at _____ Sheridan Hotel, conveniently
   located on _____ Park Avenue

   Plus a full program of tours including the following:

4. ▶ a boat trip of New York on _____ Hudson River with a stop at
   _____ Brooklyn Bridge

5. ▶ a tour to _____ Liberty Island to see _____ Statue of Liberty

6. ▶ a bus tour to _____ Wall Street with a stop at the World Trade
   Center

7. ▶ a visit to _____ Columbia University, _____ Times Square,
   _____ New York Public Library, _____ Metropolitan Museum, and
   _____ Central Park

8. ▶ a tour of _____ United Nations, located on _____ East River

9. ▶ a trip to _____ Jones Beach, the largest waterfront park on _____
   Atlantic Ocean

10. ▶ a flight to _____ Lake Placid, located in _____ northern New York
    including a visit to the place where the Winter Olympics were held in
    _____ Adirondack Mountains

11. ▶ a visit to _____ Mount Marcy, the highest point in New York

12. ▶ a flight to _____ Lake Ontario to see Niagara Falls

For more information, call
Northern Airlines (212) 555-1100

MAKE IT WORK

Name two things you would like to see in New York.

_____

_____

THE SHERIDAN IS A HOTEL.

Review: Articles

Verb *To Be*

The Sheridan is a hotel.		Fifth Avenue is a street.

PRACTICE

Classify the items in the chart. Make sentences with *the*, no article, *a,* or *an.*

The	sun Atlantic Amazon South America Golden Gate West Indies Fuji Hilton Columbia Broadway Waikiki Louvre	is	a an	hotel. museum. street. mountain. ocean. bridge. star. beach. river. university. continent. island.

1. *The sun is a star.* _____
2. _____
3. _____
4. _____
5. _____
6. _____
7. _____
8. _____
9. _____
10. _____
11. _____
12. _____

MAKE IT WORK

Name two things to see in your country.

_____   _____

ETHAN'S FATHER HANDED HIM A GIFT. THE GIFT WAS A BOOK.

Review: Articles

Past Tense

> Ethan graduated from ☐ college on │the│ 15th of June.
> His father handed him │a│ gift. │The│ gift was │a│ book.

PRACTICE

Fill in the blanks with *a, the,* or a line for no article (—).

___A___ young man from _____ rich family was about to graduate from
(1)   (2)

_____ Harvard University. _____ young man's father was very proud of
(3)   (4)

him. He decided to give him _____ car for his graduation. _____ young man,
(5)   (6)

Ethan, and his father looked at _____ cars for months. Finally, at _____
(7)   (8)

beginning of June, Ethan and his father found _____ beautiful car. Ethan was
(9)

sure _____ beautiful car would be his on graduation night.
(10)

On _____ 15th of June, Ethan graduated from _____ college. In
(11)   (12)

_____ evening after his graduation, Ethan's father handed him _____
(13)   (14)

gift. _____ gift was _____ book. At _____ first, Ethan was very
(15)   (16)   (17)

disappointed. Then he became so angry that he threw _____ book down and
(18)

ran out of _____ house. He never saw his father again.
(19)

When his father died, Ethan went _____ home. As he was sitting in his
(20)

father's living room, he saw _____ book that his father had given to him for
(21)

his graduation. He opened it and found _____ check dated _____ June 15th.
(22)   (23)

_____ check was for the exact amount of _____ car that he and his father
(24)   (25)

had chosen.

irregular past tense verbs: irregular past participles:
   become → became   choose → chosen
   find → found   give → given
   run → ran
   see → saw
   throw → threw

HE HAS A COLLECTION OF SUNGLASSES WORTH $500,000.

Affirmative Statements

Simple Present

<table>
<tr><td colspan="2" align="center">The World's Richest Singers
How Do They Spend Their Money?</td></tr>
<tr>
<td>

Name: Paul McCartney
Earnings: a personal fortune of $500 million; earns $1 million a day
Residence: a farm in Sussex, England
Ownership: a farm in Scotland

</td>
<td>

Name: Dolly Parton
Earnings: $15 million a year
Residences: houses in New York, Hollywood, Hawaii, and Nashville
Businesses: several restaurants, a $6 million amusement park called Dollywood

</td>
</tr>
<tr>
<td>

Name: Michael Jackson
Earnings: a personal fortune of $200 million
Residence: a house in Encino, California, with 50 rooms
Ownership: a private zoo

</td>
<td>

Name: Barbara Mandrell
Earnings: $10 million a year
Residence: houses in Nashville and Aspen
Possessions: a yacht, a helicopter
Businesses: a health club, a museum in Nashville

</td>
</tr>
<tr>
<td colspan="2">

Name: Elton John
Earnings: $35 million a year
Residence: a mansion built by King Henry VIII in England
Collections: an art collection worth $15 million a collection of sunglasses worth $500,000
Possessions: a Rolls-Royce, a Bently, a Ferrari

</td>
</tr>
</table>

Note: Hollywood is in California. Nashville is in Tennessee. Aspen is in Colorado.

New Words: yacht = a sailboat used for pleasure
mansion = a large house

helicopter

HE HAS A COLLECTION OF SUNGLASSES WORTH $500,000.

> Paul McCartney [earns] $1 million a day.
> He [lives] on a farm in Sussex, England.

PRACTICE

Read the profiles on page 18. Then make sentences about each singer.

1. Paul McCartney *earns $1 million a day.* _____
2. _____
3. _____
4. _____
5. Dolly Parton _____
6. _____
7. _____
8. _____
9. Michael Jackson _____
10. _____
11. _____
12. Barbara Mandrell _____
13. _____
14. _____
15. _____
16. Elton John _____
17. _____
18. _____
19. _____
20. _____

MAKE IT WORK

Name your most important possession.

_____

SHE WROTE HER FIRST BOOK AT THE AGE OF 24.

Regular and Irregular Past Tense Verbs

She **wrote** her first book at the age of 24.

regular verbs	irregular verbs	
die → die**d**	be → was/were	read → read
want → want**ed**	become → became	say → said
	come → came	spend → spent
	go → went	think → thought
	grow → grew	write → wrote
	have → had	

PRACTICE

Fill in the blanks with the past form of the verb in parentheses.

Agatha Christie, one of the most popular writers in the English language, was born in 1891 and _____*died*_____ in 1976. She _____
(1. die)   (2. grow)

up in a small town in England. She never _____ to school, but
(3. go)

she _____ a great deal when she was young. "I _____
(4. read)   (5. have)

a very lazy childhood," she once _____ . "I _____
(6. say)   (7. spend)

most of my time making up stories. It _____ a very happy life."
(8. be)

Agatha Christie _____ to write her first book because she
(9. decide)

_____ to prove that she could write a good mystery story.
(10. want)

In 1915 she _____ *The Mysterious Affair at Styles*. Six publishers
(11. write)

_____ the book, but it was finally published in 1920. After that,
(12. reject)

she _____ one mystery book a year until her death.
(13. publish)

Her private life _____ ordinary in contrast to her detective
(14. be)

stories. She _____ of most of her ideas while she was doing
(15. think)

chores around the house. "In fact," she once _____ , "some of
(16. say)

my best ideas _____ to me while I was working at the kitchen sink."
(17. come)

During her lifetime, Agatha Christie also _____ more than 70
(18. write)

detective stories; 31 of her stories _____ plays or movies.
(19. become)

But she _____ , "People think writing is easy for me. It isn't.
(20. confess)

It's murder."

MAKE IT WORK

Answer the questions.

Where did you grow up?

_____

Where did you go to school?

_____

What was your childhood like?

_____

_____

New Words: grow up = become an adult
childhood = the time when someone is a child
make up = invent
reject = not accept
ordinary = usual
confess = admit something wrong, especially a crime

I SAW A MOVIE A WEEK AGO.

Irregular Past Tense Verbs

When did you last see a movie? I saw a movie yesterday.
a month ago.

drink → drank	forget → forgot	see → saw	swim → swam
drive → drove	give → gave	send → sent	take → took
eat → ate	lose → lost	sleep → slept	wear → wore
fly → flew	ride → rode	speak → spoke	

PRACTICE

Answer the questions. Tell about yourself.

1. When did you last drink champagne?
   I drank champagne two months ago.

2. When did you last speak to a stranger?

3. When did you last drive a car?

4. When did you last take a nap?

5. When did you last eat at a fancy restaurant?

6. When did you last send someone a postcard?

7. When did you last wear something green?

8. When did you last sleep until noon?

9. When did you last ride a bicycle?

10. When did you last lose something?

11. When did you last give a party?

12. When did you last swim in the ocean?

13. When did you last forget an appointment?

14. When did you last fly on a jet?

SHE DIDN'T GO TO SCHOOL.

Past Form vs. Simple Form

She didn't go to school.
Her mother tutored her.
As a child, she liked to read.

PRACTICE

Fill in the blanks with the past form or the simple form of the verb in parentheses.

1. (grow) Agatha Christie didn't _____grow_____ up in a large city.

2. (grow) She _____ up in a small town in England.

3. (go) She didn't _____ to school.

4. (tutor) Her mother _____ her.

5. (read) Agatha Christie learned to _____ when she was very young.

6. (make) She had a vivid imagination, and she liked to _____ up stories.

7. (challenge) When she was in her twenties, Agatha's sister _____ her to write a book.

8. (accept) Agatha agreed to _____ the challenge.

9. (complete) She _____ her first novel in 1915.

10. (publish) Since she was an unknown writer, most publishers didn't want to _____ her novel.

11. (reject) Six publishers _____ the book, but it was finally published five years later.

12. (have) After that, she _____ no trouble getting her books published.

13. (have) Even though Agatha's novels are exciting, she didn't _____ an especially exciting private life. In fact, her life was rather ordinary.

14. (think) People _____ writing was easy for Agatha because she wrote so many books.

15. (think) But Agatha didn't _____ it was easy.

New Words: tutor = teach by private instruction
vivid imagination = clear, lifelike pictures in the mind
challenge = invite someone to compete

23

MR. JONES DECIDED TO CORRECT THE SITUATION.

Review: Regular and Irregular Past Tense Verbs

Mr. Jones says, "Bon appetit."		Mr. Jones said, "Bon appetit."

irregular verbs

get → got	meet → met	understand → understood
know → knew	stand → stood	swim → swam
sit → sat	tell → told	

PRACTICE

Read the story below. Then rewrite the sentences in the space on page 25. Use the past tense.

An American named Jones is on a boat trip. The first day of the trip, he sits opposite a Frenchman for lunch. The Frenchman arrives late. As he comes in, he turns to Mr. Jones and says, "Bon appetit." Mr. Jones, who knows no French at all, thinks that the Frenchman is giving his name, so he stands up and says, "Jones."

The second day the Frenchman arrives late and says, "Bon appetit." Mr. Jones gets up and says, "Jones." The third day the same thing happens.

The fourth day, as Mr. Jones is taking a morning walk around the boat, he meets an old friend. His friend asks him how the trip is going. Mr. Jones mentions that there is an Italian man named Bonappetit opposite him at lunch. His friend understands the situation immediately. He explains that the man isn't Italian. He tells Mr. Jones that the man is French and that he is wishing him a pleasant lunch. Mr. Jones decides to correct the situation.

Mr. Jones arrives late for lunch that day. When he walks into the dining area, the Frenchman is already eating. Mr. Jones says, "Bon appetit." The Frenchman smiles and says, "Jones."

MR. JONES DECIDED TO CORRECT THE SITUATION.

An American named Jones was on a boat trip.

_____

_____

_____

_____

_____

_____

_____

_____

_____

_____

_____

_____

_____

_____

_____

_____

_____

_____

_____

_____

_____

MAKE IT WORK

Practice telling the story with a classmate.
Use the past tense.

I'LL LOSE WEIGHT.

Negative and Affirmative Statements

Future with *Will*

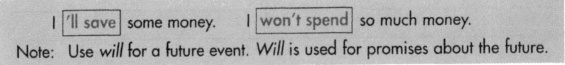

I ['ll save] some money.   I [won't spend] so much money.

Note: Use *will* for a future event. *Will* is used for promises about the future.

PRACTICE

Make ten New Year's resolutions for next year. You can use the chart below, or you can make up your own resolutions. Use contractions.

I'll I won't	lose weight. quit smoking. worry so much. exercise more. stop wasting time. work so hard. work harder. eat so fast. eat "junk" food.	be nicer to people. go to church more often. watch so much TV. save some money. spend so much money. be on time. be more organized. spend more time with my family. criticize people.

1. *I'll lose weight.* _____

2. _____

3. _____

4. _____

5. _____

6. _____

7. _____

8. _____

9. _____

10. _____

MAKE IT WORK

Write your most important New Year's resolution.

_____

Recopy it onto another piece of paper and save it for next January.

I WON'T WORK ON SUNDAYS.

Negative and Affirmative Statements

Future with *Will*

> I | 'll work | on Sundays.
>
> I | won't work | on Sundays.
>
> Note: *will* = willing to do something; *won't* = not willing to do
> something (refusal)

PRACTICE

Tell which of the following things you will do and which things you won't do.

1. wear shorts   *I'll wear shorts.*
2. eat alone at a restaurant   _____
3. fly in an airplane   _____
4. eat raw fish   _____
5. eat spinach   _____
6. sleep on the floor   _____
7. open the door for men   _____
8. ride in a boat   _____
9. lend money to friends   _____
10. walk alone at night   _____
11. listen to loud music   _____
12. ask for directions   _____
13. sit in the smoking section   _____
    at a restaurant   _____
14. sing in public   _____

New Words: raw = not cooked
           alone = without other people
            lend = give something to someone with the idea it will be returned
          public = a place where a lot of people will see you

WHEN HE'S IN ST. THOMAS, HE'LL DO SOME SHOPPING.

Statements with *After* and *When*

Future with *Will*

> Victor will leave New York. Then he'll arrive in San Juan.
>
> After Victor ⎡leaves⎤ New York, he ⎡'ll arrive⎤ in San Juan.
>
> Note: Use the present tense in clauses beginning with *after* and *when*.
> Use the future tense in the main clause.

PRACTICE

Combine the sentences with *after* or *when*. Use contractions whenever possible.

1. Victor will leave New York. Then he'll arrive in San Juan.

   After Victor leaves New York, he'll arrive in San Juan.

2. He'll see San Juan. Afterward he'll go to St. Thomas.

   _____

3. He'll be in St. Thomas. At that time he'll do some shopping.

   _____

4. He'll spend a day in St. Thomas. Then he'll go to Martinique.

   _____

5. He'll be in Martinique. At that time he'll buy some French perfume.

   _____

6. He'll be in Martinique. At that time he'll also go swimming.

   _____

7. He'll see Martinique. Then he'll go to Barbados.

   _____

8. He'll leave Barbados. After that he'll go to La Guaira.

   _____

9. He'll be in La Guaira. At that time he'll visit Caracas.

   _____

10. He'll visit Caracas. Then he'll go home.

    _____

THE COUPLE WILL LIVE IN BUCKINGHAM.

Contrast: Present, Past, Future with *Will*

PRACTICE

Fill in the blanks with the correct verb tense. Use the simple present, the simple past, or the future with *will*.

DeFazio-Cortina Wedding

The Union Church in Newtown
_____was_____ the setting for the marriage
   (1. be)
of Ashley Cortina and Robert DeFazio last Saturday.

   The parents of the couple _____ Mr. and Mrs. Arthur Cortina
                        (2. be)
of Newtown and Mr. and Mrs. Jerry DeFazio of Buckingham.

   The bride _____ a white wedding dress and _____
             (3. wear)   (4. carry)
white daisies. The bridesmaids _____ Mrs. John R. Wilson and
                        (5. be)
Julie Cortina, sisters of the bride. Linda Martino _____ the maid
                        (6. be)
of honor, and Richard Cox _____ as best man.
             (7. serve)

   The bride and groom both _____ from Newtown High School
             (8. graduate)
last June. At the present time, the bride _____ as a dental
             (9. work)
assistant in Buckingham. The groom currently _____ for the
             (10. work)
State of Pennsylvania. He _____ a part-time accountant. Next
             (11. be)
fall, Mr. DeFazio _____ Bucks County Community College where
             (12. attend)
he _____ in accounting. After a wedding trip to Jamaica, the
             (13. major)
couple _____ in Buckingham.
             (14. live)

HE WON $20.7 MILLION IN THE LOTTERY.

Contrast: Present, Past, Future with _Will_

irregular verbs: hide → hid   leave → left

DAILY NEWSPAPER

MAN WINS $20.7 IN LOTTERY

Last week, Leo Marco, age 27, won $20.7 million in the lottery in California. He learned he won the lottery while he was at work. After he heard the news, he left work early because he was too excited to work. Then he went home and hid his lottery ticket under his mattress.

Marco, originally from the Philippines, came to the United States in 1992. He lives with his mother and sister in a two-bedroom apartment, and he drives a 1988 Ford. He has a job at a minimarket and earns $16,000 a year.

Marco will use part of his lottery money to help his family in the Philippines. He'll also buy a house, and he'll give some of his money to charity. "But I won't buy a new car," Marco added. "My car is a sign of good luck."

PRACTICE

A. Read the story above. Use contractions whenever possible.

B. Tell two things that Leo Marco did the day he won the lottery.

1. _He left work early._

2. _____

C. Tell four things about Leo Marco's life in the United States.

3. _____

4. _____

5. _____

6. _____

D. Tell four things that Marco will or won't do with his lottery money.

7. _____

8. _____

9. _____

10. _____

New Words: hide = put out of sight
charity = help given to people in need

THEIR SON IS GETTING A DIVORCE. HE HAS TWO CHILDREN.

Present Continuous vs. Present

temporary action	permanent state
The Stantons' son is getting a divorce.	He has two children.

Note: Use the present continuous for an action that is temporary; use the present for a state that is permanent.

Note: Not all verbs can occur in the present continuous. Verbs of state—stative verbs—generally occur in the present. Some stative verbs are:

1. verbs of mental perception.

   believe   forget   know   remember

   understand   feel and think (when they mean *believe*)

2. verbs of preference.

   dislike   hate   hope   like   love

   need   prefer   want   wish

3. verbs of measurement.

   cost   weigh

4. verbs of relationship.

   belong (to)   contain   fit   have   own

5. linking verbs.

   be   seem

6. verbs of perception.

   feel   hear   see   smell   sound   taste

Some stative verbs can occur in the continuous if they are active or temporary in meaning.

active	stative
She 's being very nice.	She 's a nice person.
He 's having problems with his marriage.	He has two children.

31

THEIR SON IS GETTING A DIVORCE. HE HAS TWO CHILDREN.

PRACTICE

Fill in the blanks with the present continuous or the present tense. Read the entire letter before you begin. Use contractions whenever possible.

Dear Letty,

   I know it's been a long time since my last letter. Right now Bob

___*is visiting*___ his parents, and Sonia _____ at the
　　　　(1. visit)　　　　　　　　　　　　　　　　　　　　(2. shop)

mall, so I _____ some free time to write.
　　　　　　　　(3. have)

   Guess what? I _____ an ESL class at the university now.
　　　　　　　　　　　　(4. take)

I _____ class every Monday and Wednesday evening.
　　(5. have)

I _____ a lot, and I _____ my teacher is
　　(6. learn)　　　　　　　　　　　　(7. think)

excellent.

   My daughter, Sonia, _____ sixteen now, and she
　　　　　　　　　　　　　　　(8. be)

_____ a boyfriend. Her boyfriend _____ nice,
　　(9. have)　　　　　　　　　　　　　　　　　　(10. seem)

but I _____ she's too young to date.
　　　　(11. feel)

   My son, Edwin, _____ up so fast. He's in college now, and
　　　　　　　　　　　　(12. grow)

he _____ in business. It _____ a lot of money
　　　(13. major)　　　　　　　　　　　(14. cost)

to go to school here, so he's working part time after school to pay for his

education.

THEIR SON IS GETTING A DIVORCE. HE HAS TWO CHILDREN.

My husband still _____ his job at United Bank, but
                        (15. like)

he _____ the commute. He _____ to find a
        (16. dislike)   (17. want)

job closer to home.

You _____ Clara and John Stanton, don't you? They
        (18. remember)

_____ a house in Windy Bush two blocks from where we live.
    (19. own)

I _____ Clara all the time. We _____ to the
        (20. see)   (21. belong)

same health club. Their son _____ a divorce, and he will
                                    (22. get)

probably move back home again.

What's new with you? Are you working? How's your mother? Please

say "hello" to her from me.

Write soon.

Love,

Florie

MAKE IT WORK

Evaluate your English course. Tell what you like or dislike about the course
and what you think of your progress.

I think my English is improving. _____

_____

_____

_____

New Word: commute = the trip back and forth regularly

HE'S SAILING TO ST. THOMAS ON DECEMBER 1ST.

Present Continuous and Present with Future Intention

> He ｜'s flying｜ to San Juan on Monday.   He ｜flies｜ to San Juan on Monday.
>
> Note: You can use both the present continuous and the present to express future time when talking about definite plans, like schedules.

PRACTICE

A friend is going to take this cruise. Tell about his itinerary. For each item, make two sentences expressing future time. Use the present continuous and the present tense.

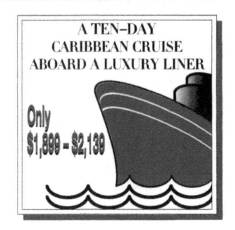

A TEN–DAY CARIBBEAN CRUISE ABOARD A LUXURY LINER

Only $1,899 – $2,139

Sail from Puerto Rico to St. Thomas on December 1st.

1. *He's sailing from Puerto Rico to St. Thomas on December 1st.*

2. *He sails from Puerto Rico to St. Thomas on December 1st.*

Stop in Antigua on December 3rd.

3. _____

4. _____

Visit Martinique on December 5th.

5. _____

6. _____

Go to Trinidad on December 8th.

7. _____

8. _____

Stay in Caracas on December 9th and 10th.

9. _____

10. _____

Fly back to Puerto Rico on December 11th.

11. _____

12. _____

New Word: cruise = a trip on a boat

TWO WOMEN AND A MAN WERE STANDING IN LINE.

Subject–Verb Agreement

Past Continuous

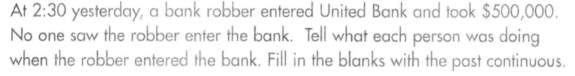

Two women and a man [were standing] in line.

The man behind the two women [was writing] a check.

Note: The verb must agree in number with the subject. If the subject is modified by a phrase that begins with a preposition, the verb usually agrees with the head word or words.

PRACTICE

At 2:30 yesterday, a bank robber entered United Bank and took $500,000. No one saw the robber enter the bank. Tell what each person was doing when the robber entered the bank. Fill in the blanks with the past continuous.

1. (talk) The bank teller _____*was talking*_____ to the woman at the teller's window.

2. (deposit) The woman at the teller's window _____ some money in her account.

3. (stand) Two women and a man _____ in line.

4. (talk) The two women standing in line _____ to each other.

5. (write) The man behind the two women _____ a check.

6. (endorse) The woman at the table near the window _____ _____ a check.

7. (fill) The men next to her _____ out deposit slips.

8. (sit) The loan officer _____ at his desk.

9. (apply) The man and woman sitting in front of the loan officer _____ for a loan.

10. (wait) The two people sitting on the couch _____ to see the loan officer.

New Words: endorse = sign your name on the back of a check
                 deposit = put in the bank
                 fill out = complete

WHILE SHE WAS WATCHING TELEVISION, HER TWO OLDEST CHILDREN CAME HOME FROM SCHOOL.

Statements with *When* and *While*

Simple Past, Past Continuous

> She | was reading | a book when the doorbell | rang.
>
> While she | was reading | a book, the doorbell | rang.
>
> Note: Use the past continuous for a long, continuing action. Use the past
> tense for an action that interrupts a longer action.
>
> irregular verbs: begin → began   ring → rang   put → put

PRACTICE

Fill in the blanks with the correct verb tense. Be sure to read each sentence first.

1. Roberta (rest) _was resting_____ when her alarm clock accidentally (go) _went_____ off.

2. She (take) _____ a bath when the doorbell (ring) _____ .

3. While she and her next-door neighbor (have) _____ coffee, the plumber (arrive) _____ .

4. The telephone (ring) _____ while the plumber (talk) _____ to her.

5. She (talk) _____ on the telephone when the baby (start) _____ to cry.

6. While she (feed) _____ the baby, she (have) _____ another telephone call.

7. She and the baby (play) _____ in the yard when it (start) _____ to rain.

8. She put the baby down for another nap. While she (eat) _____ lunch, the baby (begin) _____ to cry again.

9. While the baby (sleep) _____ , she (decide) _____ to watch television.

10. While she (watch) _____ television, her two oldest children (come) _____ home from school.

HE'S BEEN RAKING THE LEAVES FOR THREE HOURS.

Affirmative Statements

Present Perfect Continuous

> He's raking the leaves. He started three hours ago.
>
> He ⌈ **'s been raking** ⌋ the leaves for three hours.
>
> Note: The present perfect continuous is formed with *have* or *has* + *been* + verb + *ing*.
>
> For practice with *for*, *since*, and *ago*, see page 116.

PRACTICE

Combine the sentences using the present perfect continuous. Use contractions whenever possible.

1. He's mowing the lawn. He started three hours ago.

    He's been mowing the lawn for three hours.

2. She's watering the lawn. She started four hours ago.

    _____

3. They're pulling weeds. They started an hour ago.

    _____

4. She's planting flowers. She started two hours ago.

    _____

5. They're painting the house. They started six hours ago.

    _____

6. He's putting up the storm windows. He started two hours ago.

    _____

7. They're washing the windows. They started four hours ago.

    _____

8. He's fixing the driveway. He started three hours ago.

    _____

9. She's sweeping the patio. She started an hour ago.

    _____

10. He's trimming the bushes. He started three hours ago.

    _____

New Words: weed = an unwanted plant that prevents flowers from growing

trim = make neat or even by cutting

HE'LL BE EARNING $50,000 A YEAR.

Affirmative Statements

Future Continuous

> **Sales Manager $50,000 a year**
>
> Work in sales department, hire salespeople, develop a sales team, manage a sales team, and report to the president of the company. Must be able to travel ten days a month, go to conferences, give speeches, and write sales reports.
>
> Call Rick Brown (714) 555-1214

He'll be earning $50,000 a year.

Note: Use the future continuous for actions that will be in progress at a definite time in the future.

The future continuous is formed with *will + be + verb + ing.*

PRACTICE

Look at the ad above. George Benton has just been hired for the position of manager. Tell what he'll be doing in two weeks. Use contractions whenever possible.

1. _He'll be earning $50,000 a year._____

2. _____

3. _____

4. _____

5. _____

6. _____

7. _____

8. _____

9. _____

10. _____

MAKE IT WORK

Answer the question.

Next year at this time, what will you be doing?

_I'll be_____

_____

WHEN I RETURN TO THE OFFICE AT 12:30, HE'LL BE EATING LUNCH.

Review: Present, Past, and Future Continuous

It's 12:00 now. He ‍ ‍['s eating] lunch.

When I left the office at 11:30, he [was eating] lunch.

When I return to the office at 12:30, he ['ll be eating] lunch.

PRACTICE

Fill in the blanks with the correct continuous tense. Use contractions whenever possible.

It's 1:00 now. She's typing the report.

1. When I arrived at the office at 11:00, *she was typing the report.*

2. When I leave the office at 5:00, *she'll be typing the report.*

When I arrived at the office at 9:00, they were working on the report.

3. It's 10:00 now. _____

4. When the boss arrives at 11:00, _____

When I arrived at 9:00, she was sitting at the switchboard.

5. When I leave at 11:00, _____

6. It's 10:00 now. _____

It's 1:00 now. The boss is waiting for the report.

7. When I see him at 2:00, _____

8. When I saw him at 12:00, _____

It's 1:30. They're eating lunch.

9. When I see them at 1:45, _____

10. When I saw them at 1:00, _____

MAKE IT WORK

Answer the questions.

What are you doing now? _____

What were you doing an hour ago? _____

What will you be doing in an hour? _____

NO, THANKS. I'VE ALREADY HAD DINNER.

Statements with *Already* and *Yet*
Present Perfect: Irregular Past Participles

Would you like to have dinner after class?

No, thanks. I | 've already had | dinner.

Yes, I would. I | haven't had | dinner | yet |

Note: Use *already* in affirmative statements; use *yet* in negative statements.

Have been can be used in place of *have gone* in the perfect tenses.
Would you like to go to the cafeteria? Sure, I *haven't been* there yet.

irregular past participles

buy → bought	drive → driven	make → made	see → seen
choose → chosen	go → gone	meet → met	speak → spoken
do → done	have → had	read → read	

PRACTICE

Make negative and affirmative sentences with *yet* and *already*. Answer in complete sentences. Use contractions whenever possible.

1. Would you like to drive around the campus?
   No, thanks. *I've already driven around the campus.*

2. Would you care to see the new language lab?
   Yes, I would. _____

3. Would you like to choose an English class?
   No, thanks. _____

4. Would you like to make an appointment with the foreign student advisor?
   Yes, I would. _____

5. Would you like to read the student handbook?
   No, thanks. _____

6. Would you like to meet the instructor?
   Yes, I would. _____

7. Would you like to speak to the instructor after class?
   Yes, I would. _____

8. How about going to the bookstore?
   No, thanks. _____

9. Would you like to buy a dictionary?
   Good idea. _____

10. Would you like to do the homework with me?
    No, thanks. _____

I'VE NEVER HEARD EGYPTIAN MUSIC.

Statements with Never

Present Perfect: Irregular Past Participles

I 　've never been　 to Egypt. 　　 I 　've been　 to Egypt.

Note: The present perfect can be used to express an action that occurred
at an unknown time in the past.

irregular past participles

ate → eaten	flew → flown	kept → kept	swam → swum
drank → drunk	heard → heard	slept → slept	was/were → been

PRACTICE

Respond to each statement. Tell if you've ever done the following things.
Use *never* or *too* in your sentences. Use contractions whenever possible.

1. My friend was in Egypt last month. *I've never been to Egypt. OR*

   I've been to Egypt, too.

2. She flew on a supersonic jet. _____

3. She met an Egyptian. _____

4. She ate Egyptian food. _____

5. She drank mint tea. _____

6. She saw a wall painting. _____

7. She spoke Arabic. _____

8. She heard Egyptian music. _____

9. She swam in the Mediterranean. _____

10. She drove through the desert. _____

11. She slept in a tent. _____

12. She kept a diary. _____

MAKE IT WORK

Name something in your country you've never seen.

_____

New Words: Arabic = the language spoken in Egypt

　　　　　　　 mint = a plant with leaves used for flavoring

　　　　　　　 diary = a daily record of the events in someone's life

HAVE YOU EVER RIDDEN A CAMEL?

Questions with *Ever*

Present Perfect: Irregular Past Participles

> I was in Egypt. ☐Have☐ you ☐ever been☐ to Egypt?
>
> irregular past participles
>
> brought → brought   rode → ridden   stood → stood   wore → worn
> got → gotten   spent → spent   took → taken

PRACTICE

Respond to each statement by making a question with *you* (or *your*).

1. My friend was in Egypt last month.   *Have you ever been to Egypt?*
2. She spent Egyptian money.   _____
3. She went to a bazaar.   _____
4. She bought Egyptian jewelry.   _____
5. She took a boat trip up the Nile.   _____
6. She rode a camel.   _____
7. She stood in front of a temple.   _____
8. She saw the pyramids.   _____
9. She read a book on the history of Egypt.   _____
10. She got up at 4:30 to see a sunrise.   _____
11. She wore a veil.   _____
12. She brought home souvenirs of her trip.   _____

New Words: bazaar = a market with a group of shops
temple = a building dedicated to worship

veil

pyramids

sunrise

42

NO ONE IN THE CLASS HAS EVER EATEN OYSTERS.

Review: Present Perfect

Chang has met a famous person.

Gloria and Chang have met a famous person.

No one in the class has ever eaten oysters.

irregular past participles: win → won   write → written

PRACTICE

Interview your classmates. Find out who has done the following things. Then report your answers below.

1. drive a motorcycle   *No one in the class has ever driven a motorcycle.*

2. see Disneyland   _____

3. eat oysters   _____

4. ride a camel   _____

5. wear a wig   _____

6. be on TV   _____

7. climb a mountain   _____

8. win a prize   _____

9. meet a famous person   _____

                             _____

10. smoke a cigar   _____

11. write a book   _____

12. swim in the Atlantic   _____

                             _____

13. go bungee jumping   _____

14. rent a car   _____

New Words: oyster   bungee jumping   wig

BY THE TIME GARY GOT THERE, THE WEDDING RECEPTION HAD STARTED.

Affirmative Statements

Past Perfect: Regular and Irregular Past Participles

The wedding reception started at 5:00. The guests arrived between 5:00 and 5:30, and everyone had a glass of champagne. At 5:30, the bride and groom cut the cake, and everyone ate a piece of cake. At 6:00, the band started to play. Then the bride danced with the groom. At 6:30, the bride threw her bouquet. At 6:45, several people left the reception. The bride and groom left the reception shortly before 7:00.

The wedding reception started at 5:00. Gary got there at 7:00.

By the time Gary got there, the wedding reception | had started |

Note: Use the past perfect tense for a past action completed before another past action.

irregular past participles: cut → cut   left → left   threw → thrown

PRACTICE

Gary arrived at the reception at 7:00. By the time he arrived, what had happened? Make sentences using the past perfect tense.

1. _The wedding reception had ended._

2. _____

3. _____

4. _____

5. _____

6. _____

7. _____

8. _____

9. _____

10. _____

MAKE IT WORK

Did you ever arrive late at a reception, a party, a meeting, a class, or a speech? Tell one thing that had happened before you arrived.

I arrived late at _____ . By the time I arrived, _____

_____

I HADN'T BEEN TO A BASEBALL GAME IN A LONG TIME.

Negative Statements
Past Perfect: Regular and Irregular Past Participles

I went to a baseball game last night.

I hadn't been to a baseball game in a long time.

contraction: hadn't → had not

PRACTICE

Make negative sentences using the past perfect. End your sentences with *in a long time.*

1. She went to a party last night. (be)

   She hadn't been to a party in a long time.

2. They ate out last night.

   _____

3. He cleaned out the garage last weekend.

   _____

4. I saw a good movie last Saturday.

   _____

5. We went to the beach last Sunday. (be)

   _____

6. They took a vacation last week.

   _____

7. I read a good book last weekend.

   _____

8. We played miniature golf last weekend.

   _____

9. They visited their family last weekend.

   _____

10. I went to the doctor yesterday. (be)

   _____

MAKE IT WORK

Name something you did recently that you hadn't done in a long time.

I went to a concert last Thursday. I hadn't been to a concert in a long time.

_____

_____

Statements with *Already* and *Yet*

Past Perfect: Regular and Irregular Past Participles

Maria's List of Things To Do
March 20

9:00	meet with the Art Department get a report from the Sales Department
10:00	write the Avco report
12:00	type the Avco report copy the Avco report put the Avco report on Mr. Ripley's desk
1:00	lunch
2:00	send a fax to Avco open the mail
3:00	file the correspondence from yesterday
4:00	give Mr. Ripley his phone messages
4:30	meet with Mr. Ripley

New Word: fax

BY 2:00, SHE'D ALREADY EATEN LUNCH.

irregular past participles: give → given   put → put   send → sent

Maria had already met with the Art Department.

She hadn't sent a fax to Avco yet.

Note: Use *already* in affirmative statements; use *yet* in negative statements.

contractions: hadn't = had not   she'd = she had   I'd = I had

PRACTICE

Maria's boss, Mr. Ripley, arrived at the office yesterday at 2:00. Look at Maria's schedule for March 20th on page 46. Then tell what Maria had already done and what she hadn't done by the time Mr. Ripley arrived.

1. *She'd already met with the Art Department.*
2. _____
3. _____
4. _____
5. _____
6. _____
7. _____
8. _____
9. _____
10. _____
11. _____
12. _____
13. _____
14. _____

MAKE IT WORK

Answer the question.

Name three things you had already done by 12:00 yesterday.

I'd already _____

_____

_____

UNTIL LAST WEEK, MARIO HAD NEVER SEEN SNOW.

Statements with *Never*

Past Perfect: Regular and Irregular Past Participles

Mario saw snow last week.
Until last week, he ⌈ **'d never seen** ⌋ snow.

PRACTICE

Make sentences using the past perfect tense and *never*. Begin your sentences with *until last week*.

1. Mario visited the United States.

    Until last week, he'd never visited the United States.

2. He flew over the Atlantic Ocean.

    _____

3. He saw snow.

    _____

4. He spoke English.

    _____

5. He met an American.

    _____

6. He ate a hamburger.

    _____

7. He drank a milkshake.

    _____

8. He heard country music.

    _____

9. He watched an American TV program.

    _____

10. He went to a barbecue.

    _____

MAKE IT WORK

Name a place that you've visited. Then tell two things that you had never done before you visited that place.

Until I visited _____

_____

BY THE TIME THEY ARRIVE, SHE'LL HAVE COOKED THE MEAL.

Affirmative Statements

Future Perfect

> By the time they arrive, she │ **'ll have cooked** │ the meal.
>
> Note: Use the future perfect for an action that the speaker thinks will be
> completed before a specific future time.
>
> irregular past participle: set → set

PRACTICE

Rita is going to have a party. Her guests will arrive at 7:00 P.M. Look at
Rita's list below. Then tell what she'll have done by the time her guests
arrive.

> ### Rita's List of Things To Do for the Party
>
> | | |
> |---|---|
> | clean the house | cook the meal |
> | buy the food | make the punch |
> | iron the tablecloth | bake a cake |
> | set the table | change into a party dress |
> | decorate the living room | turn on the CD player |

1. _She'll have cleaned the house._
2. _____
3. _____
4. _____
5. _____
6. _____
7. _____
8. _____
9. _____
10. _____

MAKE IT WORK

Name three things you'll have accomplished by the end of this year.

_I'll have _____

_____

_____

BY JULY 1ST, SHE'D BEEN IN 20 STATES.

Review: Present, Past, and Future Perfect

> By July 1st, Cindy had been in 20 states.
>
> As of today, she 's been in 30 states.
>
> By January 1st, she 'll have been in 40 states.

Cindy's Trip

Cindy's traveling around the United States for a year. She left on January 1st. She'll return next January 1st. She's planning her itinerary very carefully. Here are her notes about her trip.

	BY JULY 1st	AS OF TODAY	BY JANUARY 1st
1.	20 states	30 states	40 states
2.	4,500 miles	6,000 miles	11,000 miles
3.	$7,000	$11,000	$14,500
4.	several friends	a dozen friends	a lot of friends
5.	no souvenirs	a few souvenirs	a lot of souvenirs
6.	no Pacific Ocean	the Pacific Ocean	the Pacific twice
7.	Niagara Falls	Niagara Falls and Disneyland	Niagara Falls, Disneyland, and the Grand Canyon
8.	90 postcards	135 postcards	180 postcards

PRACTICE

Look at page 50. Then tell about Cindy's trip. Use the past perfect, the present perfect, and the future perfect.

1. (be in)   By July 1st, she'd been in 20 states.

    As of today, she's been in 30 states.

    By January 1st, she'll have been in 40 states.

2. (drive) _____

    _____

    _____

3. (spend) _____

    _____

    _____

4. (visit) _____

    _____

    _____

5. (buy) _____

    _____

    _____

6. (see) _____

    _____

    _____

7. (go to) _____

    _____

    _____

8. (write) _____

    _____

    _____

HE'S VISITED 143 COUNTRIES SO FAR. HE VISITED 4 COUNTRIES LAST SUMMER.

Contrast: Present Perfect vs. Past

He | 's visited | 143 countries so far.   He | visited | 4 countries last summer.

PRACTICE

Fill in the blanks with the present perfect or the past tense. Use contractions whenever possible.

People have called Jesse Rosdail the world's most traveled man.

He _'s visited_____ 143 of the world's 147 countries. He also
　　　　(1. visit)

_____ to many territories and out-of-the-way islands.
　　(2. travel)

Mr. Rosdail, a fifth-grade teacher from Elmhurst, Illinois, said last week, "I

_____ to 290 islands and countries so far."
　　(3. be)

He _____ last summer visiting the Marquesas Islands.
　　　　(4. spend)

He _____ there three times before his plane could land.
　　(5. fly)

The summer before last, he _____ to the Santa Cruz Islands
　　　　　　　　　　　　　(6. go)

near New Guinea. He _____ a private plane to take him
　　　　　　　　(7. hire)

there. He also _____ the Bonin Islands near Japan. Then he
　　　　　　(8. see)

_____ to Africa, where he _____ through
　　(9. go)　　　　　　　　　　　　　　　　　　(10. drive)

Ethiopia and _____ Djibouti on the Indian Ocean.
　　　　　　(11. visit)

"It's still interesting to go to the far corners of the earth," says Rosdail.

"If there's a place I _____ to, it attracts me."
　　　　　　　　　(12. not/be)

Most people _____ outside their own countries. In fact,
　　　　　　　(13. never/travel)

they _____ of most of the places that Mr. Rosdail
　　(14. never/hear)

_____ to.
　　(15. be)

BY THE TIME THE POLICE ARRIVED, THE ROBBERS HAD ALREADY LEFT.

Contrast: Past Perfect vs. Past

Time before basic time	Basic time (Moment of speaking)	Time after basic time
Before the police arrived, the robbers had left.	The police arrived.	After the police arrived, they questioned the guard.
irregular verbs: break → broke → broken forget → forgot → forgotten		steal → stole → stolen wake → woke → woken

PRACTICE

Fill in the news article with the past perfect or the past tense.

TWO PAINTINGS STOLEN FROM ROYAL MUSEUM

A robbery _____occurred_____ last night at the Royal Museum in London.
(1. occur)

The robbers _____ in while a guard was sleeping. The guard
(2. break)

_____ up after he heard a noise. He _____ the
(3. wake)   (4. call)

police at 11:00 P.M.

By the time the police arrived, the robbers _____ . After
(5. leave)

the police arrived, they _____ the museum. They discovered
(6. search)

that the robbers _____ two paintings some time before 11:00 p.m.
(7. steal)

The police found that someone _____ to lock the back door.
(8. forget)

At 12:00, the police _____ the guard and the director of the
(9. question)

museum, William West. West said that he _____ the two paintings
(10. see)

earlier that day. He said the paintings _____ worth over $600,000.
(11. be)

No one _____ the robbers enter or leave the museum.
(12. see)

53

I HOPE SHE HAS A BOY.

Clauses After *Hope*

Do you think that Teresa will have a boy?
I hope (that) she has a boy.

Note: Use *hope* to express a desire that is expected to be fulfilled now or in the future.

PRACTICE

Make sentences with *I hope*. Use pronouns in your sentences.

1. Do you think Teresa will have a boy?

   I hope she has a boy.

2. Do you think I'll pass the examination?

   _____

3. Do you think Dennis and Mako will get married?

   _____

4. Do you think Sally will get a promotion?

   _____

5. Do you think Nick Andropolis will win the election?

   _____

6. Do you think Irving and Amy will get engaged?

   _____

7. Do you think Victor will receive an award?

   _____

8. Do you think I'll get a raise?

   _____

9. Do you think Paul will graduate from law school?

   _____

10. Do you think Andrea will be accepted to medical school?

    _____

MAKE IT WORK

Name two things you hope for now or in the future.

_____

_____

I WISH I DIDN'T HAVE TO WORK.

Clauses After *Wish*: Present Events

He doesn't have to work.	I wish (that) I didn't have to work.
He's independent.	I wish I were independent.

Note: Use *wish* + the past tense to express a desire that is not likely to be fulfilled now or in the future. With the verb *to be*, use *were* for all persons.

PRACTICE

Make sentences about yourself using *I wish*.

1. Simon doesn't have a care in the world.
   I wish I didn't have a care in the world.

2. He doesn't have to worry about money.
   _____

3. He doesn't have to buy clothes.
   _____

4. He has a beautiful fur coat.
   _____

5. He lives in a big house.
   _____

6. He's independent.
   _____

7. He doesn't have to work.
   _____

8. He can sleep until noon every day.
   _____

9. He doesn't have to be anywhere at any particular time.
   _____
   _____

10. Simon is a cat.
    _____

MAKE IT WORK

Make two wishes about your life now.

_____

_____

HE WISHES HE COULD SPEAK ENGLISH BETTER.

Review: *Hope* vs. *Wish*

> Ed can't speak English very well.
>
> He [wishes] he [could speak] English better.
>
> He [hopes] he [learns] to speak English better.
>
> **Note:** Use the past tense, *would*, or *could* after *wish*; use the present tense, *will*, or *can* after *hope*.

PRACTICE

Ed arrived in the U.S. a week ago. He is a student at the university. Make two different sentences for each item, one with *wish* and the other with *hope*.

Ed can't understand the lectures at the university.

1. *He wishes he could understand the lectures at the university.*

2. *He hopes he can understand the lectures better.*

He doesn't know any Americans.

3. _____

4. _____

He doesn't have a part-time job.

5. _____

6. _____

He doesn't have a car.

7. _____

8. _____

He doesn't live very near the university.

9. _____

10. _____

He doesn't have much money.

11. _____

12. _____

MAKE IT WORK

Make two sentences about your ability in English. Use *wish* and *hope*.

_____

_____

IF YOU BUY THREE BARS OF SOAP, YOU'LL GET ONE FREE.

Future Real Conditional

condition	result
If you ⎾present⏌ this card at our shop, you ⎾'ll get⏌ a free gift.

Note: The future real conditional is used to express a situation that is expected as a result of some condition or requirement. Use the present tense for the condition; use the future tense for the result.

You is used in general statements to mean *anyone*.

PRACTICE

Make sentences using the future real conditional. Use contractions whenever possible.

1. Buy three bars of soap. Get one bar free.

   If you buy three bars of soap, you'll get one bar free.

2. Open a new account at United Bank. Receive a free TV.

   _____

3. Buy two cans of King Tuna. Save 60¢.

   _____

4. Visit our pharmacy. Get $2.00 off on any prescription.

   _____

5. Call this number now. Get a clock radio.

   _____

6. Visit our shop. Receive a free gift.

   _____

7. Buy one chicken dinner. Get the second one free.

   _____

8. Purchase a Kobe TV now. Get 40% off.

   _____

9. Attend our grand opening. Receive a free plant.

   _____

10. Buy an airline ticket by May 1st. Get 50% off.

    _____

MAKE IT WORK

Look at the coupon. Then make a sentence using the future real conditional.

BIG TIME SUPERMARKET
30% OFF   30% OFF
COLOMBIAN COFFEE 30 - OUNCE CAN

_____

_____

IF I HAD A SWIMMING POOL, I'D GO SWIMMING EVERY DAY.

Present Unreal Conditional

> If I │had│ a swimming pool │,│ I │'d go│ swimming every day.
>
> Note: The present unreal conditional is used to express possibilities in the present.
>
> contraction: I'd = I would

P R A C T I C E

Imagine that you had or owned the following things. What would you do?
Write sentences beginning with *if*.

1. a swimming pool   _If I had a swimming pool, I'd go swimming every_
   day.

2. an airplane   _____

3. a piano   _____

4. a yacht   _____

5. a ranch   _____

6. a mansion   _____

7. a Rolls-Royce   _____

8. a horse   _____

9. a private movie theater   _____

10. a fur coat   _____

MAKE IT WORK

Answer the question.

If you had a million dollars, what would you do?

_____

IF I COULD LIVE MY LIFE OVER, I'D TAKE BETTER CARE OF MYSELF.

Present Unreal Conditional

If I | could live | my life over, I | 'd take | better care of myself.

Note: contraction: wouldn't = would not

PRACTICE

What would you do if you could live your life over? Make sentences with *would* and *wouldn't*. You can use the chart below, or you can make your own sentences. Use contractions whenever possible.

If I could live my life over,		take better care of myself.
		have more fun.
		eat desserts first.
		work 10 hours a day.
		spend more time with my family.
	I'd	finish my education.
	I wouldn't	travel.
		live my dreams.
		marry someone else.
		worry about money.
		have a lot of children.

1. *I'd have more fun.* _____
2. _____
3. _____
4. _____
5. _____
6. _____
7. _____
8. _____
9. _____
10. _____
11. _____
12. _____

IF I'D BEEN KING EDWARD OF ENGLAND, I WOULDN'T HAVE GIVEN UP MY THRONE FOR A WOMAN.

Past Unreal Conditional

If I ⌈'d been⌉ King Henry VIII, I ⌈would have had / wouldn't have had⌉ six wives.

Note: Use *if* + the past perfect tense + *would have* + the past participle for unreal possibilities in the past.

contraction: I'd = I had   irregular past participle: fought = fought

PRACTICE

If you had been each of the following people, would you or wouldn't you have done what they did? Use negative or affirmative sentences.

1. King Henry VIII had six wives.

   If I'd been King Henry VIII, I wouldn't have had six wives.
   _____

2. Thomas Becket died for his church.

   _____
   _____

3. Susan B. Anthony fought for women's rights.

   _____
   _____

4. Grace Kelly gave up her movie career to marry a prince.

   _____
   _____

5. Jean-Paul Sartre refused the Nobel Prize.

   _____
   _____

6. King Edward of England gave up his throne for a woman.

   _____
   _____

7. Joan of Arc died for her country.

   _____
   _____

8. Martin Luther King, Jr., fought for civil rights.

   _____

   _____

9. Charlie Chaplin gave up his U.S. citizenship.

   _____

   _____

10. Cleopatra killed herself.

    _____

    _____

11. Napoleon fought the Battle of Waterloo.

    _____

    _____

12. Mahatma Gandhi fasted for his political beliefs.

    _____

    _____

13. Jane Addams improved working conditions for the poor.

    _____

    _____

14. Queen Elizabeth I never got married.

    _____

    _____

15. Abraham Lincoln freed the slaves.

    _____

    _____

New Words:

give up	= leave; resign
throne	= the chair of a king or queen
Nobel Prize	= an important prize given in Sweden each year for work in science and literature
resign	= leave or quit a position
fast	= not eat any food
slave	= a person who is the property of another; a servant

IF SHE HADN'T WOKEN UP LATE, SHE WOULDN'T HAVE BEEN IN A HURRY.

Past Unreal Conditional

She woke up late. She was in a hurry.

If she hadn't woken up late , she wouldn't have been in a hurry.

Note: Use the past unreal conditional for an unreal possibility in the past.

contraction: hadn't = had not

PRACTICE

Make negative sentences in the past unreal conditional. Use contractions whenever possible.

1. She woke up late. She was in a hurry.

    If she hadn't woken up late, she wouldn't have been in a hurry.

2. She was in a hurry. She had to run to the train station.

    _____

3. She had to run to the train station. She slipped on the ice.

    _____

4. She slipped on the ice. Her briefcase opened.

    _____

5. Her briefcase flew open. Her papers were scattered everywhere.

    _____

6. Her papers were scattered everywhere. She had to pick them up.

    _____

7. She had to pick them up. She arrived at the train station late.

    _____

8. She arrived at the train station late. She missed her train.

    _____

9. She missed her train. She arrived at the office late.

    _____

10. She arrived at the office late. Her boss was angry.

    _____

New Word: scatter = separate in all directions

SHE WISHES THE GUESTS HADN'T ARRIVED EARLY.

Clauses After *Wish*: Past Events

The guests arrived early.   Margo wishes the guests hadn't arrived early.

She wasn't ready. She   wishes   she 'd been ready.

Note: Use *wish* + the past perfect tense to express a desire that did not happen in the past.

PRACTICE

Make sentences with *wish*.

1. The guests arrived early.

   Margo wishes the guests hadn't arrived early.

2. She wasn't ready.

   _____

3. She didn't have time to set the table in advance.

   _____

4. She forgot to serve the appetizer.

   _____

5. The roast wasn't done on time.

   _____

6. She burned the potatoes.

   _____

7. She spilled wine all over the tablecloth.

   _____

8. The dessert didn't turn out.

   _____

9. She wasn't able to spend time with her guests.

   _____

10. The evening was a disaster.

    _____

MAKE IT WORK

Write about an unpleasant event that happened to you in the past. Then make a wish about that event.

I lost my wedding ring.   *I wish I hadn't lost it.*

_____   _____

New Word: appetizer = something that is eaten before a meal

IF I COULD LIVE ANYWHERE I WANTED, I'D LIVE IN PARIS.

Review: Future, Present, and Past Conditionals

If I take a vacation next year, I ⟨'ll go⟩ to Paris.

If I took a vacation next year, I ⟨'d go⟩ to Paris.

If I'd taken a vacation last year, I ⟨'d have gone⟩ to Paris.

PRACTICE

Complete the sentences. Use contractions whenever possible.

1. If I could live my life over, _I'd take better care of myself._

2. If I have enough money, _____

   _____

3. If I owned a mansion, _____

   _____

4. If I'd gotten up earlier today, _____

   _____

5. If I win the lottery, _____

   _____

6. If I'd had a better education, _____

   _____

7. If I were the president of my country, _____

   _____

8. If I could live anywhere I wanted, _____

   _____

9. If I'd lived 100 years ago, _____

   _____

10. If I have some free time next week, _____

    _____

MAKE IT WORK

Compare the sentences you wrote with a classmate's.

I'D HAVE BEEN RICH IF I'D INVESTED MY MONEY WISELY.

Review: Future, Present, and Past Conditionals

> I'll go to Paris if I [take] a vacation next year.
>
> I'd go to Paris if I [took] a vacation next year.
>
> I'd have gone to Paris if I ['d taken] a vacation last year.

PRACTICE

Complete the sentences.

1. I'll buy a new car if *I have enough money.* _____

2. I'd be surprised if _____

3. I'd have been rich if _____

   _____

4. I'll be happy if _____

5. I'd have retired last year if _____

   _____

6. I'll be disappointed if _____

7. I'd be in debt if _____

8. I'd have taken a cruise last year if _____

   _____

9. I'd go on a diet if _____

10. I'd be lonely if _____

11. I'll return to my country if _____

    _____

12. I'd change jobs if _____

    _____

MAKE IT WORK

Compare the sentences you wrote with a classmate's.

New Words: invest = put money into something with the purpose of future profit

be in debt = owe money to someone

I SHOULD DO MY HOMEWORK, BUT I'D RATHER READ A BOOK.

Should vs. Would Rather

I | should do | my homework, but I | 'd rather | read a book.

Note: Use *would rather* to express a preference where a choice is given.
Use *should* to show that an action is advisable in the present or future.

contraction: I'd = I would

PRACTICE

Look at each choice of activities. First tell what you *should* do. Then tell what you'*d rather* do. Join your sentences with a comma (,) and *but*.

1. read a book/do my homework

   I should do my homework, but I'd rather read a book.

2. do the laundry/go to the movies

   _____

3. watch the baseball game/clean the house

   _____

4. mow the lawn/take a nap .

   _____

5. fix dinner/go out

   _____

6. stay in bed/get up early

   _____

7. drink a glass of water/have some soda

   _____

8. do the dishes/watch television

   _____

9. stay home/go to work

   _____

10. go to a party/do my work

   _____

MAKE IT WORK

Make one sentence about this weekend. First tell what you *should* do. Then tell what you'*d rather* do instead.

_____

YOU MUST NOT GET UP AND WALK AROUND.

Have To, Don't Have To, and Must Not

You | have to | fasten your seat belt.

You | must not | get up and walk around.

You | don't have to | fasten your seat belt.

Note: *have to* and *must* = obligation
must not = prohibition
don't have to = lack of necessity

PRACTICE

Fill in the blanks with *have to*, *don't have to*, or *must not*. Read the entire sentence first.

1. You _____ *have to* _____ be at the airport early to reserve a seat. Otherwise, you might not get a seat on the plane.

2. You _____ check large suitcases. You can't carry them on the plane.

3. You _____ check your briefcase or purse. You can carry hand luggage on the plane if you like.

4. You _____ put your hand luggage under your seat or in the overhead compartment.

5. You _____ leave anything in the aisles.

6. You _____ fasten your seat belt when the plane takes off and lands.

7. You _____ get up and walk around when the "FASTEN YOUR SEAT BELT" sign is on.

8. You _____ keep your seat belt fastened the entire time. You can get up and walk around after the "FASTEN YOUR SEAT BELT" sign goes off.

9. You _____ smoke on flights within the United States.

10. You _____ see the movie. You can if you want to.

MAKE IT WORK

Name one important rule for a passenger who flies on an airplane.

You _____

New Words: reserve = keep for future use
entire = whole

aisle

67

SHE COULD TAKE A NAP.

Opportunity with *Could*

Phil is hungry.
There's chicken and hamburger in the refrigerator.

He | could have | chicken.

Note: Use *could* to show that an opportunity
exists in the present or future.

PRACTICE

Make two sentences for each item. Use *could.*

Anna is sleepy.
1. *She could take a nap.*
2. *She could drink some coffee.*

Rafael and Gloria are bored.
3. _____
4. _____

Dennis is broke.
5. _____
6. _____

Akira is lonely.
7. _____
8. _____

John and Marie are lost.
9. _____
10. _____

Julia is in trouble.
11. _____
12. _____

MAKE IT WORK

John is broke. He has no money to go out Saturday night. What are some
things he could do that don't cost any money?

He could watch TV.

_____

_____

IT COULD BE A RAINBOW. IT MIGHT BE A RAINBOW.

Possibility with *Could* and *Might*

What is this?    It could be a rainbow.

It might be a rainbow.

Note: Use *could* or *might* for possibility.

PRACTICE

What could each of the following items be? Suggest two different possibilities for each item. Make one sentence with *could* and another with *might*.

1. *It could be a package with a bow.*

2. *It could be a shirt with a bow tie.*

3. _____

4. _____

5. _____

6. _____

7. _____

8. _____

9. _____

10. _____

MAKE IT WORK

Compare your sentences with a classmate's. Then check your answers on page 141.

THEY SHOULDN'T HAVE SOLD THEIR PIANO.

Past Advice with *Should Have*

> She's sorry she didn't marry Rolly Green.
>
> She │ should have married │ Rolly Green.
>
> She's sorry she married Walt Bennett.
>
> She │ shouldn't have married │ Walt Bennett.
>
> Note: Use should (or *shouldn't*) + *have* + the past participle to express an action that was advisable in the past, but didn't occur.
>
> irregular verbs: quit → quit   sold → sold
>
> (For additional practice, see page 87.)

PRACTICE

Make sentences with *should have* or *shouldn't have*. Begin your sentences with a pronoun.

1. Leonard is sorry he didn't finish high school.

   He should have finished high school.

2. Marie is sorry she married Tom.

   _____

3. Dorothy is sorry she didn't marry Rolly Green.

   _____

4. Tish and Jack are sorry they didn't invest their money wisely.

   _____

5. Brian is sorry he didn't save more money.

   _____

6. Stacey is sorry she quit her job.

   _____

7. Bruce and Susan are sorry they sold their piano.

   _____

8. Louise is sorry she didn't learn to drive.

   _____

9. Diane is sorry she cut her hair.

   _____

10. Gina and Tony are sorry they bought such an expensive house.

    _____

MAKE IT WORK

Name one thing you should have done but didn't.

_____

SHE COULD HAVE HAD AN ACCIDENT.

Past Possibility with *Could Have*

> I stepped on a piece of glass.   You could have cut your foot.
>
> Note: Use *could have* + the past participle for past possibility.
>   *Might have* can also be used for past possibility.
>
> irregular past participles: catch → caught   hurt → hurt
>   fall → fallen   shoot → shot

PRACTICE

Make sentences with *could have* and the words in parentheses.

1. I stepped on a piece of broken glass. (cut your foot)

   You could have cut your foot.

2. She climbed the broken ladder. (fall off the ladder)

   _____

3. He went outside in the snow without his jacket. (catch a cold)

   _____

4. I moved the furniture by myself. (hurt your back)

   _____

5. She didn't stop at the traffic light. (have an accident)

   _____

6. He crossed the street against the light. (be hit by a car)

   _____

7. The children were playing with a gun. (shoot someone)

   _____

8. They skied down the icy hill. (get hurt)

   _____

9. She turned on the radio with her wet hands. (get a shock)

   _____

10. The little boy went swimming by himself. (drown)

   _____

New Words: shock = the effect of electricity passing through your body

   drown = die by being underwater for a long time

71

SHE USED TO LIVE WITH HER PARENTS.

Used To

I don't live with my parents anymore.　I used to live with my parents.
She doesn't collect coins anymore.　She used to collect coins.
Note: *Used to* expresses a recurring action in the past.

PRACTICE

Make sentences with *used to.*

1. She doesn't live in a small town anymore.
   She used to live in a small town.

2. She doesn't live with her parents anymore.

3. She doesn't play with dolls anymore.

4. She doesn't wear cowboy hats and blue jeans anymore.

5. She doesn't dress up in her mother's clothes anymore.

6. She doesn't climb trees anymore.

7. She doesn't play baseball in the street anymore.

8. She doesn't collect stamps anymore.

9. She doesn't take ballet lessons anymore.

10. She doesn't read comic books anymore.

MAKE IT WORK

Answer the question.

What used to be true about you that isn't true now?
I used to live with my parents.

YOU DIDN'T USE TO LIKE SPINACH.

Didn't Use To

You | didn't use to wear | glasses.

Note: Omit the *d* in *use to* when you make negative statements.

PRACTICE

Make negative responses with *used to*. Begin your sentences with *you*.

1. I like spinach. _You didn't use to like spinach._
2. I drink coffee. _____
3. I smoke a lot. _____
4. I like to be alone. _____
5. I read a lot. _____
6. I wear glasses. _____
7. I enjoy classical music. _____
8. I like concerts. _____
9. I like modern art. _____
10. I enjoy serious discussions. _____
11. I like foreign films. _____
12. I like to study. _____

MAKE IT WORK

Answer the question.

What's true about you now that didn't use to be true?

I didn't use to be talkative.

_____

HE ISN'T USED TO LIVING IN THE CITY.

Be Used To

> Tony lived in the suburbs.   He isn't used to living in the city.
>
> Note: Use the verb *to be* + *used to* + verb + *ing* to describe actions
>   that a person has (or hasn't) become accustomed to.

PRACTICE

Tony used to live with his parents in the suburbs. Now he lives in the city
and has a job. Fill in the blanks with *be used to* and the appropriate verb.

1. Tony lived in the suburbs.

   He isn't used to living _____ in the city.

2. He didn't work.

   _____ from 9:00 to 5:00.

3. He commuted to school by bus.

   _____ to work by car.

4. He lived with his parents.

   _____ alone.

5. He lived in a house.

   _____ in an apartment.

6. His mother cooked all his meals.

   _____ all his own meals.

7. His mother cleaned the house.

   _____ his apartment.

8. His mother did the laundry.

   _____ the laundry.

9. His parents supported him.

   _____ himself.

10. He didn't pay his own bills.

    _____ his own bills.

MAKE IT WORK

Fill in the blanks with a form of *be used to*. Tell about yourself.

_____ living in a big city.

_____ supporting myself.

New Words: suburb = the outer area of a city
                 support = provide money for a person to live

74

COULD YOU HAVE LEFT IT IN YOUR POCKET?

Contrast: Simple Form vs. Past Participle

simple form	past participle
should + take	should have + taken
have to + take	must have + taken
didn't + take	haven't + taken
did (you) + take	have (you) + taken

Note: irregular past participle: lay → laid

PRACTICE

Fill in the blanks with the correct form of the verb in parentheses.

Amanda: I lost my ring.

Debbie: Where did you _____*put*_____ it?
(1. put)

Amanda: I don't know. I was washing the dishes in the kitchen.

Debbie: Well, then it must _____ in the kitchen.
(2. be)

Amanda: It isn't there. I must have _____ it down somewhere else.
(3. lay)

Debbie: Is it in the bathroom? It could _____ there.
(4. be)

Amanda: No. I checked the bathroom. I took it off, but I can't _____
where I put it.
(5. remember)

Debbie: How about your pocket? Could you have _____ it in your
pocket?
(6. leave)

Amanda: No. I looked.

Debbie: You should _____ every place that you've been today.
(7. look)

Amanda: I have _____ everywhere. It's lost. I shouldn't have
(8. look)

_____ it off.
(9. take)

Debbie: I'd like to _____ you find it, but you mustn't _____
(10. help)   (11. get)

upset. You have to _____ calm. Let's _____
(12. stay)   (13. make)

a list of every place you've been today. I'm sure we'll

_____ it.
(14. find)

New Words: lay down = set down or place
take off = remove

75

YOU SHOULDN'T HAVE DRIVEN HOME.

Review: Modals and Idiomatic Modals

I had three glasses of wine at a party, and I'm going to drive my car home from the party.

You shouldn't drive home.   You could have an accident.

I had three glasses of wine at a party, and I drove my car home from the party.

You shouldn't have driven home.   You could have had an accident.

PRACTICE

Read each situation. Then make an appropriate response with either a present or past form of *could* or *should*. Begin your sentences with *you*.

1. I left my jacket somewhere. I was at work all day. After work, I went to school. Where did I leave my jacket? Give a possibility.

   You could have left it at work.
   _____

                    OR

   You could have left it at school.
   _____

2. I know that smoking is bad for my health, but I smoke anyway. Give me some advice.

   _____

3. My husband and I went to a restaurant. It was very crowded, and we had to wait for a table for an hour. Give us some advice.

   _____

4. I'm going to Europe next year. Give me some advice about what countries to go to.

   _____

5. I didn't study for my Spanish test, and I failed it. Give me some advice.

   _____

6. My husband and I don't have much money, but we want to watch a movie tonight. Give a possible solution to our problem.

   _____

7. I have a test at school tomorrow, but I'm going to a party. Give me some advice.

    _____

8. Susan and Bruce invited me to dinner at 7:00, but I arrived at 8:00. The dinner was burned. Give me some advice.

    _____

9. The weather forecast says that it'll rain today. Give me some advice about what to wear to work.

    _____

10. I had three glasses of wine at a party, but I drove home anyway. Was there another way for me to get home from the party? Give a possibility.

    _____

11. I'm going to Mexico next year. I don't know any Spanish. Give me some advice.

    _____

12. It is dinner time. I'm hungry. There are some eggs and some milk in the refrigerator. What would be a good meal for me to fix? Give a possibility.

    _____

MAKE IT WORK

Name one thing you should do this weekend.

_____

Name one thing you have to do this weekend.

_____

Name one thing you might do this weekend.

_____

Name one thing you should have done last weekend but didn't.

_____

Name one thing you could have done last weekend but didn't.

_____

GREEK OLIVE OIL AND OLIVES ARE EXPORTED ALL OVER THE WORLD.

Passive Present

> Olives are grown in Greece.
>
> irregular past participle: grow → grown

PRACTICE

Read the sentences below. Then write about your country.

	Greece
Location:	Greece is located in southeastern Europe. It's surrounded by water on three sides.
Capital city:	Athens is the capital of Greece, and it's also the largest city.
Language:	Greek is spoken in Greece, and the ancient Greek alphabet is still used.
Crops:	Grapes and olives are Greece's main crops. They are grown in the southern part of Greece.
Products:	Olive oil and wine are made in Greece.
Exports:	Olive oil and olives are exported all over the world.
Imports:	Coal is imported in Greece because there is very little coal in the country.

Location: _____

Capital city: _____

Language(s): _____

Crops: _____

_____

Products: _____

_____

Exports: _____

_____

Imports: _____

_____

MAKE IT WORK

Tell a classmate about your country.

IT'S BEING WRITTEN NOW.

Affirmative Statements

Passive Present Continuous

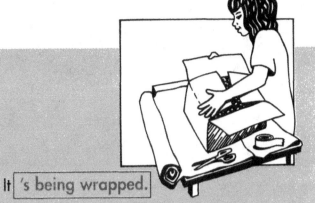

It's wrapped.   It 's being wrapped.

Note: Use *am*, *is*, or *are* + *being* + the past participle to form the passive present continuous.

PRACTICE

Answer the questions. Use the passive present continuous. Use contractions whenever possible.

1. Where's the package? (wrap)   *It's being wrapped.*
2. Where are the letters? (type)   _____
3. Where's the coffee? (make)   _____
4. Where's the mail? (open)   _____
5. Where's the brochure? (print)   _____
6. Where are the sales figures? (add) _____
7. Where are the supplies? (deliver) _____
8. Where's the memo? (copy)   _____
9. Where are the letters? (sign)   _____
10. Where are the checks? (send)   _____
11. Where's my folder? (use)   _____
12. Where's the letter? (write)   _____

MAKE IT WORK

Look at the picture and tell what's happening. Use the passive present continuous.

The check _____

_____

New Word: brochure = a small pamphlet or booklet

79

THE HOUSE WAS BUILT IN 1841.

Passive Past

The house | was built | in 1841.

It | wasn't built | for a rich family.

Note: To form the passive past, use *was* or *were* + the past participle.

irregular past participle: build → built

PRACTICE

Fill in the blanks with the passive past. Use contractions whenever possible.

The house in the picture above _____*was built*_____ in 1841. It looks very
                                          (1. build)

elegant, but it _____ for a rich family. It _____
                    (2. not/build)   (3. build)

for a middle-class family. It _____ by an architect. The style
                                    (4. not/design)

_____ from several other houses in the area.
     (5. copy)

Today, this beautiful house is an expensive apartment building, but it

_____ as an apartment building a hundred years ago. It
    (6. not/use)

_____ for one family. Originally it _____ as it is
    (7. design)   (8. not/paint)

today. The door had a beautiful design, but the design _____ in
                                                              (9. remove)

1970. The area above the door _____ of brick. It
                                     (10. not/make)

_____ of marble. In 1970, when the house _____
    (11. make)   (12. buy)

by its present owner, all the windows _____ . In fact, in 1970,
                                             (13. replace)

the entire house _____ . At that time, many old features of the
                      (14. remodel)

house _____ with newer, more modern features. Still, the
           (15. replace)

old house is elegant and charming.

New Words: remove = take away
                 marble = a hard, polished stone
                 remodel = rebuild in a new form
                 replace = remove an old item and put something new in its place

DINNER WILL BE SERVED AT 8:00.

Passive Future

> We will provide transportation to the meeting.
>
> Transportation to the meeting | will be provided. |
>
> Note: The passive future is formed with *will* + *be* + the past participle.
>
> irregular past participle: hold → held

PRACTICE

Change the sentences to the passive future.

1. The company will hold a sales meeting on September 10th.
   A sales meeting will be held on September 10th.

2. We will hold the meeting at the Manor Hotel.
   _____

3. We will expect all salespeople to attend.
   _____

4. We will provide transportation.
   _____

5. We will discuss sales from 9:00 to 11:00.
   _____

6. Someone will give a sales report from 11:00 to 12:00.
   _____

7. We will serve lunch from 12:00 to 1:00.
   _____

8. We will divide the people into two groups from 2:00 to 4:00.
   _____

9. We will give a cocktail party at 5:00.
   _____

10. The hotel will serve dinner at 8:00.
    _____

MAKE IT WORK

The president of your company says to you, "We will hold an important meeting tomorrow at 3:00 in the conference room. I will expect all employees to attend. Send a memo." Write a memo.

TO: All Employees
FROM: The President

_____

_____

HER SUPERVISOR WAS NOTIFIED ABOUT THE ACCIDENT.

Contrast: Passive Past vs. Past

> Her supervisor |was notified| about the accident.
>
> The doctor |notified| her supervisor about the accident.
>
> Note: Use the passive voice when you don't know who performed the action or when the actor is not as important as the action.
>
> *By* is sometimes used with the passive voice: Her supervisor was notified *by the doctor.*
>
> Use the active voice when the person who performed the action is important.
>
> irregular verb: hit → hit → hit

PRACTICE

Fill in the blanks with the passive past or the past tense.

As Mrs. Katz was walking to work one morning, she _____*was hit*_____ by

(1. hit)

a car. A person who happened to be walking by _____ the

(2. see)

accident and _____ an ambulance. Within minutes the ambulance

(3. call)

_____ , and Mrs. Katz _____ to the hospital.

(4. arrive)   (5. rush)

At the hospital, a doctor _____ her, and an X-ray _____ .

(6. examine)   (7. take)

Mrs. Katz _____ badly. Her arm _____ ,

(8. not/injure)   (9. bruise)

but it _____ . The doctor _____ her to go

(10. not/break)   (11. tell)

home and rest. Her supervisor at work _____ about the accident.

(12. notify)

MAKE IT WORK

Tell about an accident you had.

_____

_____

New Word: bruised = injured by a blow but not broken

82

I HAVE MY TEETH CHECKED ONCE A YEAR.

Causatives: *Have*

Regular and Irregular Past Participles

> I | have | my hair | cut | once a month.
> twice a month.
> once every six months.

Note: To form the causative, use *have* or *has* + noun or pronoun + the past participle.

PRACTICE

Answer the questions in complete sentences. Tell about yourself.

1. How often do you have your hair cut?

   I have my hair cut once every six months.

2. How often do you have a prescription filled?

   _____

3. How often do you have your clothes dry-cleaned?

   _____

4. How often do you have your watch repaired?

   _____

5. How often do you have your teeth checked?

   _____

6. How often do you have your eyes examined?

   _____

7. How often do you have your passport renewed?

   _____

8. How often do you have your car serviced?

   _____

9. How often do you have a new key made?

   _____

10. How often do you have your shoes repaired?

   _____

MAKE IT WORK

Answer the questions.

Do you have your apartment or house cleaned, or do you clean it yourself?

_____

Do you have your newspaper delivered, or do you buy it at a newsstand?

_____

VARIETY SHOWS ARE MORE ENTERTAINING.

Adjective Comparatives

Simple Present

> Documentaries and the news are both educational.
>
> I think the news is | more educational. |
>
> Note: For most two-syllable adjectives that end in *y*, change *y* to *i* and add *er*.
> funny → funnier
>
> Put *more* before adjectives with three or more syllables.
> educational → more educational
>
> Notice that *news* takes a singular verb. the news *is*

PRACTICE

Make comparative sentences. Begin your sentences with *I think that*.

1. Variety shows and game shows are both entertaining.
   I think that game shows are more entertaining.

2. Situation comedies and cartoons are both funny.
   _____

3. Talk shows and documentaries are both educational.
   _____

4. Situation comedies and variety shows are both amusing.
   _____

5. Commercials and game shows are both silly.
   _____

6. Documentaries and the news are both informative.
   _____

7. Old movies and soap operas are both interesting.
   _____

8. Mystery stories and horror movies are both terrifying.
   _____

9. Sports programs and crime dramas are both exciting.
   _____

10. Situation comedies and crime dramas are both popular.
    _____

MAKE IT WORK

	11 MOVIE *OVER THE HILL*	
8:00 P.M.	2 DAN SLICK, P.I. CRIME DRAMA	
	7 MOVIE *CASABLANCA* (1942) DRAMA	
	8 THE RACE FOR FIRST PLACE	

Tell which show you'd watch at 8:00 and why you'd watch it.

I'd watch _____ *because* _____

IT HAS THE MOST EXCITING ROLLER COASTER RIDE IN THE WORLD.

Adjective Superlatives

Simple Present, Future with *Will*

It has ⌐the most exciting⌐ roller coaster ride in the world.

Note: Add *est* to most one-syllable adjectives: great → greatest   big → biggest

Add *est* to most two-syllable adjectives ending in *y*. mighty → mightiest

Put *the most* before adjectives with three or more syllables.
exotic → the most exotic

irregular superlative form: good → the best

PRACTICE

Fill in the blanks with the correct superlative form.

You will have _____*the greatest*_____ experience of your life at Wonder
(1. great)

World Amusement Park. It is _____ amusement park in
(2. large)

the world.

It has sixty of _____ and _____
(3. mighty)   (4. exotic)

animals in the world. Wonder World has _____ roller
(5. exciting)

coaster ride in the world. It even takes you through water.

It has one of _____ hot-air
(6. big)

balloons in the United States. It's over ten stories high.

It has _____ acrobats you will ever
(7. brave)

see. It also has _____ and
(8. tall)

_____ Ferris wheel in the world.
(9. spectacular)

IT HAS THE MOST EXCITING ROLLER COASTER RIDE IN THE WORLD.

It's over twenty stories high, and it gives you a view of one of

_____ parks in the United States.
        (10. pretty)

It has one of _____ restaurants. It has
                    (11. fantastic)

everything from _____ steaks in the world
                        (12. delicious)

to _____ hot dogs in America.
            (13. good)

_____ day of your life is only minutes
        (14. wonderful)

away. The price for an entire day at Wonder World Amusement

Park is only $34.95. (It's also _____
                                        (15. expensive)

amusement park in the world!)

MAKE IT WORK

Make up an advertisement for each of the following products. Use the superlative forms (*est* or *the most*).

Ready Cola is the most refreshing drink of all.

_____

_____

_____

_____

_____

_____

_____

_____

_____

_____

HE SHOULD HAVE PRACTICED LONGER.

Adverb Comparatives

Should Have

Did he run fast enough?　　　No. He should have run 　faster.

Did he play skillfully enough?　No. He should have played 　more skillfully.

Note:　To form the comparative, add *r* or *er* to one-syllable adverbs.
　　　　Put *more* before adverbs with two or more syllables.
　　　　irregular comparative form:　well → better
　　　　irregular past participle:　run → run

PRACTICE

Make sentences with *should have* and the correct comparative form. Begin your answers with *no.*

1. Did he practice for the tennis match long enough?
   No. He should have practiced for the tennis match longer.

2. Did he hit the ball hard enough?

3. Did he hit the ball carefully enough?

4. Did he go to the net quickly enough?

5. Did he run fast enough?

6. Did he serve accurately enough?

7. Did he play skillfully enough?

8. Did he go to the net frequently enough?

9. Did he concentrate hard enough?

10. Did he play well enough?

New Words:　match = a game where people compete
　　　　　　　concentrate = have complete attention

net　　　　　　　　　　　　　　　serve

87

THERE WAS NO ELECTRICITY IN QUEENS.

Any, No, and the Pronoun *None*

Simple Present, Simple Past

> There wasn't | any | electricity in Queens.
>
> There was | no | electricity in Queens.
>
> There was | none. |
>
> Note: Use *no* and *any* before nouns; use *none* in place of a noun.
> Do not use *no* or *none* after a negative word. Use *any.*

PRACTICE

Fill in the blanks with *any, no,* or *none.*

Sally: I'm sorry I couldn't come to work yesterday. There was
         _____no_____ subway service in Queens.
             (1)

Boss: What? Why wasn't there _____ subway service?
                                        (2)

Sally: Didn't you hear? There wasn't _____ electricity in Queens.
                                              (3)

Boss: You mean there was _____ electricity in the subway?
                                   (4)

Sally: That's right. There was _____ . There wasn't
                                        (5)

         _____ power at my house, either.
              (6)

Boss: That's unbelievable. You mean there wasn't _____
         electricity in the stores?   (7)

Sally: There was _____ .
                         (8)

Boss: Not _____ electricity?
                  (9)

Sally: _____ at all. There was a total power failure in Queens.
              (10)

Boss: Wasn't there _____ way for you to get to work?
                            (11)

Sally: I don't have a car. I had _____ way to get here.
                                          (12)

MAKE IT WORK

Tell whether you have or you don't have the following items with you now.

change   _____

gum   _____

tissues _____

88

THERE'S NEVER ANYTHING FOR ME.

Any, No, Never, and Ever

Simple Present, Simple Past

incorrect	correct
There wasn't no mail today.	There wasn't $\boxed{\text{any}}$ mail today.
	There was $\boxed{\text{no}}$ mail today.
There's never nothing for me.	There $\boxed{\text{isn't ever anything}}$ for me.
	There's never $\boxed{\text{anything}}$ for me.

Note: Do not use *no, nothing, no one,* or *never* with other negative words.
       never = not ever

PRACTICE

Look at the dialogue. There are eight errors altogether. Circle the seven remaining errors. Then correct the errors, and rewrite the dialogue below.

Loi: There was(n't no) mail in the mailbox.

Julia: There wasn't no mail today.

Loi: What? You mean there wasn't no mail delivery?

Julia: No. I mean there wasn't no mail for you today.

Loi: I never get nothing in the mail.

Julia: That's because you don't never write to no one.

Loi: That's not true. It's because no one never writes to me.

Corrected Dialogue

1. Loi: *There was no mail in the mailbox.* _____

2. Julia: _____

3. Loi: _____

4. Julia: _____

    _____

5. Loi: _____

6. Julia: _____

7. Loi: _____

    _____

MAKE IT WORK

Answer the question.

How many letters did you get in the mail yesterday?

_____

THAT DRESS LOOKS GOOD ON YOU.

Adjective vs. Adverb

Simple Present

incorrect	**correct**
That dress looks well on you.	That dress looks good on you.
It fits perfect.	It fits perfectly.

Note: Use *ly* adverbs after most verbs; use adjectives after the verbs below.

be	feel	look	seem	smell	sound	taste

PRACTICE

Look at the dialogues below. There are seven errors altogether. Circle the six remaining errors. Then rewrite your corrected sentences below.

- ■ I can't play the piano very well.
- ☐ Yes, you can. You play beautiful.

- ■ Dance with me.
- ☐ I can't dance very good.
- ■ That's not true. You're the best dancer I know.
- ☐ Do you really think so? I always thought I danced bad.

- ■ I feel terribly today.
- ☐ You don't look badly. In fact, you look well.

- ■ Thank you so much for the beautiful slippers. They fit perfect.

Corrected Sentences

1. *You play beautifully.*

2. _____

3. _____

4. _____

5. _____

6. _____

7. _____

MAKE IT WORK

A friend is wearing a new suit. Compliment him on his suit.

_____

AIR POLLUTION COMES FROM AUTOMOBILES, BUSES, AND TRUCKS.

Compound Subjects and Objects

Simple Present, Present Continuous

Air pollution comes from automobiles `and` buses.

Air pollution comes from automobiles, buses, `and` trucks.

Note: Both subjects and objects can be joined in the following way:
two items: _____ *and* _____ ;
three items or more: _____ `,` _____ `,` *and* _____ .

PRACTICE

Combine the sentences.

1. Air pollution is a serious problem in almost every country. Water pollution is a serious problem in almost every country. Noise pollution is a serious problem in almost every country.

   Air pollution, water pollution, and noise pollution are serious problems in
   almost every country.

2. Air pollution comes from incinerators. Air pollution comes from smokestacks.

   _____

3. It also comes from automobiles. It also comes from buses. It also comes from trucks.

   _____

   _____

4. Water pollution comes from chemical waste. Water pollution comes from trash.

   _____

   _____

5. People throw trash into our rivers. People throw trash into our lakes. People throw trash into our oceans.

_____

6. Factories dump chemical waste into our water. Factories dump oil into our water. Factories dump detergents into our water.

_____

_____

7. Noise pollution comes from cars. Noise pollution comes from car horns. Noise pollution comes from subways.

_____

_____

8. Construction work can cause noise pollution, too. Loud radios can cause noise pollution, too.

_____

9. Our world is becoming unhealthy for people. Our world is becoming unhealthy for animals.

_____

10. However, people can do something about it. However, companies can do something about it. However, the government can do something about it.

_____

_____

MAKE IT WORK

Answer the questions.

Where does air pollution come from in your city?

_____

What are the reasons for water pollution in your city?

_____

New Words: dump = drop or unload something carelessly

 incinerator

 smokestack

chemical waste

HE DIDN'T MAKE A GOOD IMPRESSION IN THE INTERVIEW, SO MR. SIMON ISN'T GOING TO HIRE HIM.

Compound Sentences with *And, But,* and *So*

Buzz can't type | **, and** | he can't take shorthand.

Kim can type | **, but** | she can't use a computer.

Carlos is the most qualified | **, so** | Mr. Simon is going to hire him.

Note: The word *but* shows a contrast to the first part of the sentence.
The word *so* shows the result of the first part of the sentence.

PRACTICE

Buzz, Kim, Mary, and Carlos all applied for a secretarial position. Mr. Simon interviewed all of them, and this is what he thinks.

Combine the sentences with *and, but,* or *so*.

1. Buzz can use a computer. He can't type very well.

    Buzz can use a computer, but he can't type very well.

2. He can't take shorthand. He doesn't have any experience.

    _____

3. He didn't make a good impression in the interview. Mr. Simon isn't going to hire him.

    _____

    _____

4. Kim can type. She can't use a computer.

    _____

5. She was pleasant and polite in the interview. Mr. Simon isn't going to hire her.

    _____

    _____

6. She can't take shorthand. She doesn't have any experience.

    _____

7. Mary can type. She can use a computer.

    _____

8. She can take shorthand. She doesn't have any experience.

   _____

9. She didn't make a good impression in the interview. Mr. Simon isn't going to hire her.

   _____

   _____

10. Carlos can take shorthand. He can type.

    _____

11. He can use a computer. He can't use a fax machine.

    _____

12. He was pleasant and polite in the interview. He has a lot of experience.

    _____

    _____

13. Carlos is the best person for the job. Mr. Simon is going to offer the job to Carlos.

    _____

    _____

MAKE IT WORK

Give your occupation. Then tell about your skills and abilities in your field. Use *and, but,* or *so.*

I'm an electrician. I had experience in my country, but I don't have any
experience in the United States.

_____

_____

_____

_____

_____

_____

BECAUSE RUBY WORKS HARD, SHE DESERVES A PROMOTION.

Adverbial Clauses with *Because* and *Although*

Simple Present, Future with *Going To*, Present Perfect

> **Because** Irma has been with the company for many years, she deserves a promotion.
>
> **Although** Irma has been with the company for many years, she doesn't deserve a promotion.
>
> > Note: Words like *because* and *since* show result; *although* and *even though* show contrast.
> > punctuation: Because _____ [,] _____ .
> > Although _____ [,] _____ .

PRACTICE

Combine the sentences with *because* or *although*.

1. Irma has been with the company for many years. She doesn't deserve a promotion.

   Although Irma has been with the company for many years, she doesn't
   deserve a promotion.

2. Ruby hasn't been with the company for very long. She deserves a promotion.

   _____

   _____

3. Ruby works hard. She deserves a promotion.

   _____

4. Irma doesn't work hard. She doesn't deserve a promotion.

   _____

5. Irma always gets to work on time. She doesn't finish her work.

   _____

6. Ruby is sometimes late to work. She always finishes her work.

   _____

7. Irma doesn't always finish her work. She doesn't deserve a promotion.

   _____

   _____

8. Ruby is the best employee. She's going to get a promotion.

   _____

I DON'T LIKE PEOPLE WHO COMPLAIN ALL THE TIME.

Essential Adjective Clauses with *Who*

Simple Present

adjective clause

I don't like people | who talk a lot. |

Note: An adjective clause modifies a noun or pronoun in the main clause of a sentence. *Who, which,* or *that* introduces an adjective clause. Use *who* (or *that*) to refer to people.

PRACTICE

Complete the sentences with adjective clauses introduced by *who.*

1. I like people _who are good listeners._____

2. I dislike people _____

3. I notice people _____

4. I admire people _____

5. I don't trust people _____

6. I don't understand people _____

7. I feel uncomfortable with people _____

8. I don't approve of people _____

9. I get angry at people _____

10. I enjoy being around people _____

11. I'm impressed by people _____

12. I'm bored by people _____

MAKE IT WORK

Fill in the blanks with a main clause and an adjective clause.

I _____ men _____ .

I _____ women _____ .

I _____ children _____ .

New Words: admire = have respect for

trust = believe in the honesty of

approve of = consider good

impress = fill with admiration

I LIKE HOUSES WHICH ARE EASY TO CLEAN.

Essential Adjective Clauses with *Which* or *That*

Simple Present

> I like houses | which are easy to clean.
>
> I like furniture | that is easy to take care of.
>
> Note: Use *that* or *which* for things.
> Notice that the verb in this type of adjective clause
> refers back to the word it modifies.
>
> houses which *are*   furniture that *is*

PRACTICE

Make sentences with adjective clauses introduced by *which* or *that*.
Begin your sentences with *I like*.

1. houses   *I like houses which are easy to clean.*
2. furniture
3. cities
4. architecture
5. clothes
6. jewelry
7. food
8. desserts
9. cars
10. entertainment
11. books
12. video games
13. parties
14. hotels

MAKE IT WORK

Name three things you don't like. Use *which* or *that* in your sentences.

_____

_____

_____

97

I LIKE WAITERS WHO ARE PLEASANT.

Essential Adjective Clauses: *Who* vs. *Which*

Simple Present

I like restaurants which have good service.

I like waiters who are pleasant.

Note: Use *who* to introduce adjective clauses about people; use *which* to introduce adjective clauses about things.

PRACTICE

Make sentences with adjective clauses introduced by *who* or *which*. In order to practice *who* or *which*, do not use *that* in your sentences.

1. restaurants   *I like restaurants which have good service.*

2. food

3. waiters

4. salesclerks

5. department
   stores

6. movies

7. movie stars

8. singers

9. music

10. classes

11. teachers

12. apartment
    buildings

13. landlords

14. sports events

15. athletes

16. politicians

17. weather

New Word: politician = a person involved in politics, usually someone
holding an office in government

MY FORTUNE SAYS THAT I WILL TAKE A TRIP SOON.

Pronouns in Indirect Speech

My fortune says that I will take a trip soon.

Chang's fortune says that an old friend will bring him good news.

PRACTICE

Change the sentences to indirect speech.

1. You will meet someone new within a week.
   My fortune _says that I will meet someone new within a week._

2. You will get married and be happy.
   Marie's fortune _____

3. Someone has a pleasant surprise for you.
   Mohsen's fortune _____

4. You will receive a lot of money.
   My fortune _____

5. You will change your employment soon.
   Loi's fortune _____

6. You will receive something new this week.
   Gloria's fortune _____

7. An old friend will bring you good news.
   My fortune _____

8. An unexpected event will bring you money.
   Rafael's fortune _____

9. You will have many pleasures ahead.
   My fortune _____

10. You will take a long trip soon.
    Oscar's fortune _____

MAKE IT WORK

Answer the question.

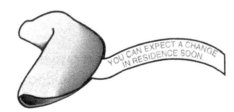

What does your fortune say?

_____

HE TOLD THE POLICE THAT HE WAS AT THE PARK ALL AFTERNOON.

Say vs. *Tell*

direct speech

He said,   "I can't tell you the exact time."

He said to the police, "I can't tell you the exact time."

indirect speech

He said   that he couldn't tell them the exact time.

He told the police that he couldn't tell them the exact time.

Note: Use *say* or *tell* with indirect speech.
          Use *say* with the exact words of the speaker.
          Use *say* without an indirect object or with *to* + indirect object.
          Use *tell* with an indirect object without *to*.

          Use *tell* with the expressions below.
           tell the truth   tell a lie   tell a story   tell the time

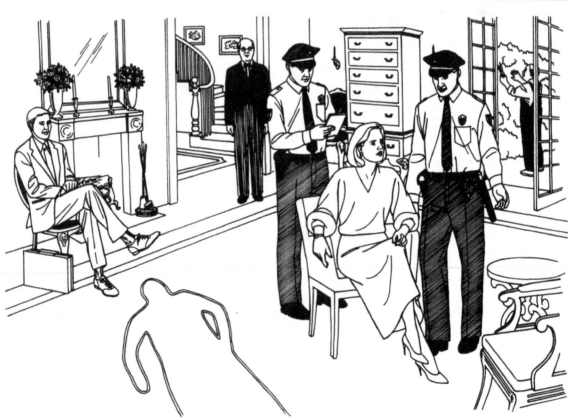

New Words: show up = arrive
                 will = the document that tells what a person wants to happen with his or her money or property after the person dies

HE TOLD THE POLICE THAT HE WAS AT THE PARK ALL AFTERNOON.

PRACTICE

Mrs. Mendoza was found dead at her house at 3:15. The police questioned the servants, the lawyer, and Mrs. Mendoza's family. This is what each person said. Fill in the blanks with *said* or *told*.

1. The lawyer _____said_____ to the police, "I had an appointment with Mrs. Mendoza at 3:00."

2. He _____ the police that Mrs. Mendoza was planning to change her will.

3. Then the lawyer _____ , "When I walked into the study, I found her lying on the floor."

4. The butler _____ the police that Mrs. Mendoza's lawyer arrived exactly at 3:00.

5. Hector Mendoza _____ them that he was at the park all afternoon.

6. The butler _____ the police that Hector left the house at about 12:00 and returned at 3:00.

7. Elvira Mendoza _____ that she was at the hairdresser's.

8. The chauffeur _____ the police that he drove Elvira to the hairdresser's at 2:00.

9. The hairdresser _____ Elvira had an appointment at 2:00, but she didn't show up.

10. The gardener _____ the police that he saw a man arrive at the house at about 2:50.

11. He _____ the police, "I don't wear a watch, so I can't tell you the exact time."

12. Paco Mendoza _____ the following story: "I was sleeping in my room. All of a sudden I heard a strange noise in the study."

13. The maid _____ that Paco was in his room from 1:00 to 2:45.

14. One of the officers said, "I think one member of the family _____ a lie."

15. He also said, "The others probably _____ the truth."

MAKE IT WORK

Which member of the family told a lie? How do you know?

_____

_____

_____

THE DOCTOR TOLD MRS. MURPHY NOT TO WORRY.

Indirect Speech: Infinitive Phrases from Imperatives

The doctor said to Mrs. Murphy, "Relax."

The doctor told Mrs. Murphy to relax.

The doctor said to Mrs. Murphy, "Don't worry."

The doctor told Mrs. Murphy not to worry.

Note: Negatives are formed by placing *not* before the infinitive.

PRACTICE

Mrs. Murphy is sick. This is what the doctor said to Mrs. Murphy. Change the direct speech to indirect speech.

1. The doctor said to Mrs. Murphy, "Drink lots of liquids."

   The doctor told Mrs. Murphy to drink lots of liquids.

2. The doctor said to Mrs. Murphy, "Don't drink any alcohol."

   _____

3. The doctor said to her, "Get lots of rest."

   _____

4. The doctor said to her, "Go to bed early at night."

   _____

5. The doctor said to her, "Don't go back to work for a week."

   _____

6. The doctor said to her, "Don't smoke any cigarettes."

   _____

7. The doctor said to her, "Don't eat rich food."

   _____

8. The doctor said to her, "Come in for a checkup next week."

   _____

9. The doctor said to her, "Take one spoonful of medicine twice a day."

   _____

10. The doctor said to her, "Don't worry."

    _____

MAKE IT WORK

The last time you went to the doctor, what did he or she tell you to do?

_____

_____

SHE TOLD HIM NOT TO PUT HIS ELBOWS ON THE TABLE.

Indirect Speech: Infinitive Phrases from Imperatives

Joe's mother said to him, "Clean up your room."

Joe's mother told him to clean up his room.

His mother said to him, "Don't put your elbows on the table."

His mother told him not to put his elbows on the table.

Note: Negatives are formed by placing *not* before the infinitive. Use *told* with an indirect object without *to*.

PRACTICE

When Joe was a child, these are the things his mother always told him. Change the direct speech to indirect speech. Be sure to change the pronouns if necessary.

1. She said to him, "Don't put your elbows on the table."

   She told him not to put his elbows on the table.

2. She said to him, "Don't talk with your mouth full."

   _____

3. She said to him, "Eat everything on your plate."

   _____

4. She said to him, "Don't eat between meals."

   _____

5. She said to him, "Stand up straight."

   _____

6. She said to him, "Don't put your feet on the furniture."

   _____

7. She said to him, "Be polite to adults."

   _____

8. She said to him, "Put your toys away."

   _____

9. She said to him, "Don't cross the street alone."

   _____

10. She said to him, "Don't talk to strangers."

    _____

HER MOTHER TOLD HER THAT SHE WAS TOO YOUNG TO GET MARRIED.

Indirect Speech: Noun Clauses from Statements

Barbara is 17 years old. She wants to get married next month. Below are some comments about her plans to get married.

Her mother said to her, "You're too young to get married."

Her father said, "You can't get married until you're 18."

Her brother said, "You're making a big mistake."

Her sister said, "Your boyfriend isn't good enough for you."

The minister said, "You can't get married without your parents' consent."

The judge said, "You need your parents' consent."

Her grandmother said to her, "You're being very foolish."

Her uncle said to her, "You'll be sorry later."

Her aunt said to her, "You haven't known him long enough."

Her grandfather said, "Your boyfriend won't be able to support you."

Her uncle said to her, "You'll be sorry later."

Her uncle said (that) she'd be sorry later.

Her father said, "You can't get married until you're 18."

Her father said (that) she couldn't get married until she was 18.

(The word *that* is optional.)

Note: When you report another person's words, change the pronouns as well as the verb tense.

will → would

present tense → past tense

present perfect tense → past perfect tense

HER MOTHER SAID THAT SHE WAS TOO YOUNG TO GET MARRIED.

PRACTICE

Below is a letter to the newspaper from Barbara's friend. Look at page 104. Make sentences with indirect speech. Use pronouns to refer to Barbara.

Dear Lorna:

My friend Barbara wants to get married. She is 17 years old, and she is still in

high school. Her mother said that _she was too young to get married._
_____
(1)

Her father said that _____ . Her
(2)

sister said that _____ .
(3)

Her brother said that _____ .
(4)

Her grandmother said that _____ .
(5)

Her uncle said that _____ .
(6)

Her aunt said that _____ .
(7)

Her grandfather said that _____
(8)

_____ . The minister said that _____
(9)

_____ . Even the judge said that
(10)

_____ .

She loves her boyfriend, and she wants to get married. What should she do?

Sincerely yours,
Barbara's Friend

Dear Barbara's Friend:

Barbara already has enough advice from her family.

New Words: consent = permission
foolish = not wise, without good sense

BILL JONES CALLED AND SAID HE WOULDN'T BE IN TODAY.

Indirect Speech: Noun Clauses from Statements

Bill Jones said, "I don't feel well."   Bill Jones said (that) he didn't feel well.

He said, "I won't be in today."   He said (that) he wouldn't be in today.

> Note: When you report another person's words, change both
> the pronouns and the verb tense.
> Present tense usually changes to past tense.
> can → could   will → would

PRACTICE

Look at each telephone message. Then complete the sentence to report the message. Use indirect speech.

"Hello. This is Bill Jones. I don't feel well. I won't be in today."

1. Bill Jones called and said _he didn't feel well._

2. He said that _____

"Hi. This is Irma Sutter. Tell Mr. Travers I'll be late this morning. I'll be in at 10:30."

3. Irma Sutter called. She said that _____

4. She said _____

"This is Jim Brown from Washington. I need the report right away. It's urgent."

5. Jim Brown called. He said _____

6. He said that _____

"It's Sue from the sales department. I'm very busy today. The report won't be ready until tomorrow."

7. Sue from the sales department called. She said that _____

_____

8. She said _____

"Saul Jacobs here. I can't come to the meeting today. I'll call back later."

9. Saul Jacobs called. He said _____

10. He said _____

THE INTERVIEWER ASKED DIANE IF SHE COULD BEGIN TOMORROW.

Indirect Speech: Noun Clauses from Yes-No Questions

The interviewer asked Diane, "Can you begin tomorrow?"

The interviewer asked Diane if she could begin tomorrow.

Note: Use *if* (or *whether*) with yes-no questions in indirect speech.
Notice that question word order changes to statement word order.
Remember to change present tense to past tense.
can → could   will → would

PRACTICE

Change the direct questions to indirect questions.

1. "Can you speak Spanish?" the interviewer asked Diane.

   The interviewer asked Diane if she could speak Spanish.

2. "Can you use a computer?" the interviewer asked Diane.

   _____

3. "Do you have any office experience?" he asked Diane.

   _____

4. He asked Diane, "Will you work overtime?"

   _____

5. "Are you a high school graduate?" he asked her.

   _____

6. "Will you work at night?" he asked her.

   _____

7. "Can you take shorthand?" the interviewer asked her.

   _____

8. He asked, "Do you have any references?"

   _____

9. "Will you work on Saturdays?" the interviewer asked.

   _____

10. The interviewer asked Diane, "Can you begin tomorrow?"

   _____

New Word: reference = written information about someone's work
experience or character

THE INTERVIEWER ASKED DIANE HOW FAST SHE COULD TYPE.

Indirect Speech: Noun Clauses from Information Questions

The interviewer asked Diane, "How fast can you type?"

The interviewer asked Diane how fast she could type.

Note: Notice that question word order changes to statement word order. Remember to change present tense to past tense, past and present perfect to past perfect, *can* to *could*, and *will* to *would*. In informal speech, the past tense is sometimes used in place of the past perfect tense.

PRACTICE

Change the direct questions to indirect questions.

1. The interviewer asked Diane, "Where do you live?"

    The interviewer asked Diane where she lived.

2. He asked Diane, "How many languages can you speak?"

    _____

3. The interviewer asked Diane, "How fast can you type?

    _____

4. "What high school did you graduate from?" he asked Diane.

    _____

5. He asked her, "When did you graduate from high school?"

    _____

6. He asked her, "How much office experience have you had?"

    _____

7. "How long did you work for Selby Company?" he asked her.

    _____

8. "How fast can you take shorthand?" he asked Diane.

    _____

9. He asked Diane, "Why do you want to work for A.B.C. Company?"

    _____

10. "When can you begin work?" he asked her.

    _____

I CAN'T BELIEVE HE ASKED HER IF SHE WAS HAPPILY MARRIED.

Review: Indirect Speech: Noun Clauses from Questions

The interviewer asked Diane, "Are you happily married?"

I can't believe the interviewer asked Diane | if | | she was | happily married.

He asked her, "Why don't you have any children?"

I can't believe he asked her | why | | she didn't have | any children.

PRACTICE

Here are some personal questions the interviewer asked Diane. Change the direct questions to indirect questions. Begin each indirect question with *I can't believe*.

1. He asked her, "Are you married?"

   I can't believe he asked her if she was married.

2. He asked her, "Are you happily married?"

   _____

3. He asked her, "Do you have any children?"

   _____

4. "Why don't you have any children?" he asked her.

   _____

5. He asked her, "Are you planning on having a family?"

   _____

6. "How much money does your husband make?" he asked her.

   _____

7. He asked her, "How old are you?"

   _____

8. "What religion are you?" he asked her.

   _____

9. He asked her, "What political party do you belong to?"

   _____

10. He asked her, "Do you have any personal problems?"

    _____

New Word: party = group or association

SOMEONE BROKE INTO HIS APARTMENT.

Indefinite Pronouns

Simple Past

> Someone broke into his apartment.
>
> Nothing was missing.
>
> There wasn't anything broken.
>
> Note: Use *someone* (or *somebody*) for people and *something* for things. *Some* and *no* are used with positive verbs; *any* is used with negative verbs. *No one* is two words. All other indefinite pronouns are one word.

PRACTICE

Fill in the blanks with *someone, something, anyone, anything, no one,* or *nothing.*

When Gus got home, it was very late at night. The street was deserted.

_____No one_____ was around. He walked into his apartment building.
　　　(1)

There were no people in the lobby. He didn't see _____ in the
　　　　　　　　　　　　　　　　　　　　　　　　　　　　　　(2)

halls either. The door of his apartment was open, but _____
　　　　　　　　　　　　　　　　　　　　　　　　　　　　　　　(3)

was there. The lock on his door was damaged, but _____ else
　　　　　　　　　　　　　　　　　　　　　　　　　　　　　(4)

in the apartment was broken. He looked around the apartment. Fortunately,

he discovered that _____ of value was missing.
　　　　　　　　　　　(5)

He called the police, and they sent _____ over right away. Gus
　　　　　　　　　　　　　　　　　　　　　(6)

explained that _____ had broken into his apartment. A police
　　　　　　　　　(7)

officer looked around the apartment building for the robber, but she didn't find

_____ . She told Gus to put _____ heavy
　　　(8)　　　　　　　　　　　　　　　　　　　　　　(9)

against the door and have a new lock put on his door quickly. There wasn't

_____ else the police officer could do for him, so she left.
　　　(10)

110

WHOSE JEWELRY WAS STOLEN?

Who's vs. Whose

Simple Present, Present Continuous, Simple Past

> | Whose | jewelry was stolen?
>
> | Who's | a suspect in the robbery?
>
> Note: *Whose* shows possession.
> *Who's* is a contraction for *who is*.

PRACTICE

An hour ago, a house in a wealthy suburb was robbed. The person who lives in the house is missing, and so is all of the money in the safe. Some jewelry, including a diamond ring, is also missing.

Fill in the blanks with *whose* or *who's.*

1. _____*Whose*_____ house was robbed?

2. _____ the owner of the house?

3. _____ missing?

4. Was the person _____ house was robbed home at the time?

5. _____ money was stolen?

6. _____ diamond ring was it?

7. _____ jewelry was in the safe?

8. _____ a suspect in the robbery?

9. Is the person _____ missing a suspect?

10. _____ fingerprints are on the safe?

11. _____ investigating the robbery?

12. _____ the robber?

MAKE IT WORK

You are a police officer investigating the robbery. Ask two important questions.

_____

_____

New Words: safe = a metal box with a lock used to protect valuable things
suspect = a person who is believed to be guilty
fingerprint = the mark of a finger, especially used in solving crimes
investigate = examine the reasons for something

THERE ARE NO LIGHTS ON. THEY'RE NOT AT HOME.

They're, There, and the Possessive Adjective *Their*
Simple Present, Present Continuous, Simple Past

> | There | are no lights on.
>
> | Their | porch light isn't on either.
>
> | They're | not at home.

Note: *There* often replaces the subject. It is usually followed by the verb *to be* in statements. *Their* shows possession. *They're* is a contraction for *they are.*

PRACTICE

Fill in the blanks with *there, their,* or *they're.*

Linda: ___There___ are no lights on. _____ not at home.
  (1)   (2)

Fred: What? _____ expecting us for dinner! Are you sure this is
  (3)

the Millers' house?

Linda: Yes, of course. _____ house is tan, and _____ are big
  (4)   (5)

trees in the front yard.

Fred: I don't think this is _____ house. _____ is a fence in
  (6)   (7)

front of _____ house.
  (8)

Linda: Yes. You're right.

Fred: What's _____ address?
  (9)

Linda: 2562 Mountainview Road.

Fred: _____ must be a mistake. This is 2562 but this isn't
  (10)

_____ house. Are you sure we're on the right street?
  (11)

Linda: I'm not positive. It's dark, and _____ are no street lights.
  (12)

Fred: Didn't the street sign say Mountain Road?

Linda: Yes.

Fred: What's the name of _____ street again?
  (13)

Linda: Mountainview.

Fred: No wonder _____ not at home. This is the wrong street.
  (14)

HE PUT HIS PAW INTO THE FISHBOWL.

Prepositions of Place and Direction

Simple Past

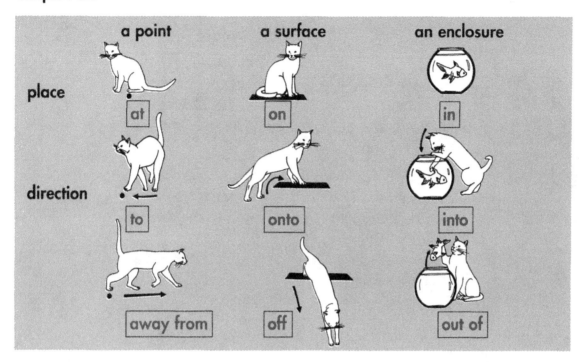

PRACTICE

Fill in each blank with one of the prepositions above.

The cat waited _____*at*_____ the door. Then he walked _____ the

(1)   (2)

table. A fishbowl was _____ the table. There was a fish _____

(3)   (4)

the fishbowl. The cat jumped _____ the table. He put his paw

(5)

_____ the fishbowl. Suddenly he pulled the fish _____ the

(6)   (7)

fishbowl and ate it. He jumped _____ the table. Then he ran

(8)

_____ the table.

(9)

MAKE IT WORK

Look at the picture. Then tell what happened.

bird cage

_____

_____

_____

_____

_____

113

HE'LL STAY IN QUITO FROM MONDAY TO WEDNESDAY.

Prepositions of Time and Place

Future with *Will*

	time		place
in	1995 January the winter the evening the afternoon the morning	in	Quito Ecuador the center of town
on	Tuesday Wednesday night January 20th the evening of January 20th	on	Tenth Street Seventh Avenue
at	6:00 noon night midnight	at	47–16 Tenth Street
from	5:00 to 6:00	from Lima to Cuzco	

Note: Use *in* with months, seasons, and years.
Use *on* with days.
Use *at* with the time of day.
Use *from . . . to* (or *until*) with a beginning time (or day) and an end time (or day).

Use *in* for cities and countries.

Use *on* with street names.
Use *at* with addresses.

Use *from . . . to* with a beginning point and an end point.

HE'LL STAY IN QUITO FROM MONDAY TO WEDNESDAY.

PRACTICE

Ken is going to South America for a week. Fill in the blanks with *in*, *on*, *at*, or *from . . . to*.

1. He'll travel to South America _____in_____ January, when it's warm and pleasant.

2. He'll arrive _____ Bogotá, Colombia, _____ Saturday, January 16th.

3. He'll arrive _____ 6:00 _____ the morning.

4. He'll stay at the Tequendama Hotel, located _____ 10-42 Twenty-sixth Street.

5. _____ Sunday, he'll visit the National Museum _____ Seventh Avenue.

6. He'll fly _____ Bogotá _____ Quito, Ecuador, the next day.

7. When he's _____ Quito, he'll visit a lot of beautiful cathedrals.

8. He'll stay in Quito _____ Monday _____ Wednesday.

9. _____ Wednesday evening, he'll fly to Lima, Peru.

10. He'll stay _____ the modern part of the city.

11. _____ the morning _____ Thursday, he'll visit the National Museum of Art.

12. _____ noon, he'll take a plane to the city of Cuzco, where he'll spend the night.

13. The next morning _____ exactly 7:10, he'll take a train _____ Cuzco _____ Machu-Picchu.

14. He'll spend the night _____ Machu-Picchu.

15. _____ the morning of January 23rd, he'll fly _____ Machu-Picchu _____ Lima. From Lima, he'll take a plane back to the United States.

MAKE IT WORK

You are going to take a vacation for a week. Tell where you'll go, when you'll leave and return, and how long you'll stay.

_____

_____

_____

SHE'S BEEN WORKING THERE FOR FIVE YEARS.

For, Since, and Ago

Simple Past, Present Perfect

> Ashley started working at Selby Company five years ago.
>
> She's been working there for five years.
>
> She's been working there since 1991.
>
> Note: Use *since* with a beginning time. Use *for* and *ago* with a period
> of time. Notice that the word order is reversed.
>
> for five years   five years ago

PRACTICE

Fill in the blanks with *for, since,* or *ago.*

1. Fernando started working at Selby Company eight years ____ago____ .

2. He's been working there _____ 1988.

3. _____ three years, Fernando worked as Assistant Sales Manager.

4. Then, five years _____ , he became Sales Manager.

5. He was Sales Manager _____ four years.

6. He was promoted to Vice-President ten months _____ .

7. He's been Vice-President _____ last March.

8. Ashley has also been working at Selby Company _____ 1991.

9. She's been working there _____ five years.

10. _____ a year she worked as a secretary in the Sales Department.

11. Four years _____ she was promoted to Assistant Sales Manager.

12. She was Assistant Sales Manager _____ three years.

13. Eight months _____ after Fernando became Vice-President, Ashley
    was promoted to Sales Manager.

14. She's had this position _____ last May.

15. She's been Sales Manager _____ about eight months.

MAKE IT WORK

Tell about your job. Tell when you started working, how long you've been
working there, and any promotions you've had.

_____

_____

_____

116

EVERYONE LAUGHED AT HIS JOKE.

Verb + Preposition

Simple Past, Past Continuous

at	about (or) of	for	to
look	think	wait	listen
glance	talk	look	pay attention
laugh	speak		talk
smile	dream		speak

Note: Some verbs occur with more than one preposition:
look at (something or someone) = watch (something or someone)
look for = try to find
talk to someone = someone is the listener
talk about something = something is the subject of the talk

PRACTICE

Fill in the blanks with *at*, *about*, *for*, or *to*.

1. The man stepped onto the platform and smiled _____*at*_____ the crowd.

2. Then he looked _____ the crowd.

3. He took the microphone and talked _____ the crowd.

4. The people listened _____ him very carefully.

5. They thought _____ his ideas.

6. They were looking _____ answers to their problems.

7. The man spoke _____ the problems in the country, but he didn't say very much.

8. He told a joke, and then he waited _____ the crowd to laugh.

9. Everyone laughed _____ his joke.

10. A woman asked a question, but he didn't pay attention _____ her.

11. He quickly glanced _____ his watch.

12. Then the man waved to the crowd and smiled. He had always dreamed _____ being a famous politician.

New Words: platform

microphone

SHE'S NEVER SURE OF THE CORRECT ANSWER.

Adjective + Preposition

Simple Present, Future with *Will*

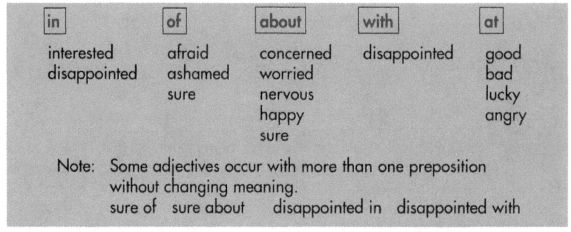

in	of	about	with	at
interested	afraid	concerned	disappointed	good
disappointed	ashamed	worried		bad
	sure	nervous		lucky
		happy		angry
		sure		

Note: Some adjectives occur with more than one preposition without changing meaning.
sure of   sure about   disappointed in   disappointed with

PRACTICE

Fill in the blanks with *in, of, about, with,* or *at*.

1. Tiffany is going to take a three-hour exam next week, and she's very nervous ____*about*____ taking it.

2. It's a math exam. She's good _____ math, but she's bad _____ taking exams.

3. She's never sure _____ the correct answer.

4. She always changes her mind and is worried _____ the choices she makes.

5. She isn't very lucky _____ guessing the correct answer either.

6. Her problem is that she's afraid _____ taking an exam.

7. She's concerned _____ failing before she's even taken the exam.

8. After the exam is over, she'll be disappointed _____ herself.

9. If she doesn't do well on the exam, she'll be ashamed _____ he score.

10. If she does well on the exam, she won't be happy _____ her score. She'll be angry _____ herself because she didn't do better.

MAKE IT WORK

Name something you're worried or nervous about.

_____

Name something you're afraid of.

_____

I SOMETIMES DREAM ABOUT TENNIS.

Review: Prepositions

Simple Present, Future with *Will*

PRACTICE

Fill in the blanks with *in, on, at, about, of,* or *to.*

I'm not very good _____*at*_____ tennis, but I love the sport. I live, eat, and

(1)

breathe tennis. _____ night, I sometimes dream _____ tennis.

(2) (3)

When the weather is good, I play tennis three times a week. I play at the

high-school courts _____ Philadelphia, Pennsylvania. _____

(4) (5)

Monday, I play _____ the afternoon. Every Wednesday I begin practice

(6)

_____ 10:00 and end _____ noon. I also take tennis lessons

(7) (8)

once a week. _____ the winter months, when it's too cold to play,

(9)

I think _____ tennis. I talk _____ my friends about tennis.

(10) (11)

I look _____ tennis matches on television. I learn a lot by watching

(12)

other people play.

Some of my friends are worried _____ me. They think I'm too

(13)

interested _____ tennis. They're tired _____ listening

(14) (15)

_____ my tennis stories. But I'll never stop talking _____ tennis.

(16) (17)

MAKE IT WORK

Answer the questions.

What sport are you interested in? Are you good at this sport or bad at it?

_____

How often do you play this sport?

_____

I LOOK FORWARD TO HEARING FROM YOU.

Verb Forms After Infinitives and Prepositions
Simple Present, Future with *Will*

> I am interested in | renting | a room.
>
> I would like to | move | in on September 1st.
>
> Note: Use the *ing* form of the verb after prepositions:
> interested *in renting*   look forward *to seeing*   worried *about renting*
> Do not use the *ing* form with verb + infinitive combinations:
> have *to find*   want *to see*   expect *to pay*   used *to live*

PRACTICE

Fill in the blanks with the correct form of the verb.

Dear Sir or Madam:

I am replying to your advertisement in the *Gazette* for a furnished room. I plan on _____studying_____ at the university this fall, and I am interested in
(1. study)

_____ a room near the campus. I expect to _____
(2. find)   (3. start)

school on September 15th and would probably need to _____ in
(4. move)

around the first week of September. I want to _____ a single room
(5. rent)

with a private bath if possible. I am interested in _____ between
(6. spend)
$90.00 and $100.00 a week.

I do not have any references because I have always lived at home. If you are

concerned about _____ a reference, I can get a reference from a
(7. obtain)

former employer. I used to _____ at Blue Bell Nursery in Los Angeles.
(8. work)

I will be in Berkeley on August 18th. I would like to _____ the
(9. see)

apartment when I am there. I look forward to _____ from you.
(10. hear)

Sincerely yours,
Yoichi Hata

New Words: furnished = with furniture   obtain = get

120

BEFORE YOU BEGIN A HOMEWORK ASSIGNMENT, YOU SHOULD LOOK IT OVER.

Separable Two-Word Verbs

Simple Present, *Should*

	noun or pronoun object	particle	noun object only
You should fill		in	the blanks.
You should fill the blanks		in.	
You should	fill · them	in.	

Note: When using separable two-word verbs, use an object pronoun before the particle but not after it.

Two-word verbs: figure out = solve   hand in = submit
fill in = write information   look up = search for
in spaces   information
talk over = discuss

PRACTICE

Fill in the blanks with one of these two-word verbs and a pronoun.

cross out   figure out   hand in   throw away
✔ look over   look up   read over   talk over

1. Before you begin a homework assignment, you should ___*look*___ ___*it*___ ___*over*___ .

2. If you don't understand a word, you should _____ _____ _____ in the dictionary.

3. If you make a mistake, you can erase it or _____ _____ _____ neatly.

4. If you don't know an answer, you should first try to _____ _____ _____ yourself.

5. If you still don't know an answer, you can _____ _____ _____ with a friend or the teacher.

6. If your homework assignment looks messy and confusing, you should probably _____ _____ _____ .

7. When you are finished with your assignment, you should always _____ _____ _____ to make sure you haven't made any mistakes.

8. If an assignment is due on Wednesday, you should _____ _____ _____ on Wednesday, not Thursday.

9. You should save all your homework assignments. You shouldn't _____ _____ _____ until the course is over.

121

DO YOU WANT ME TO TYPE IT UP TODAY?

Separable Two-Word Verbs

Simple Present

> Hand   out copies to everyone.
>
> Do you want me to | hand them out | to everyone today?
>
> Note: two-word verbs: run off   =   duplicate
>   do over   =   do again
>   hand out   =   distribute
>   turn in   =   submit   call up   =   telephone

PRACTICE

Make questions with direct object pronouns. Begin your questions with *do you want me to*.

1. Do over the sales report.   *Do you want me to do it over today?*

2. Fill in the chart.

3. Look up the information.

4. Add up the figures.

5. Write down the total.

6. Type up the report.

7. Run off fifty copies.

8. Hand out copies to all the salespeople.

9. Call up Mr. Suzuki.

10. Turn in the original copy to Mr. Suzuki.

MAKE IT WORK

Look at the dialogue. Then correct Gloria's mistake.

Boss: This report has two mistakes.

Gloria: I'm sorry. Do you want me to do over it?

SHE PICKED IT OUT.

Separable Two-Word Verbs
Simple Past

incorrect	correct
She picked out it.	She picked it out.

Note: two-word verbs:
- hang up = place on a hanger
- make out = write
- pick out = select
- put on = dress; put on one's body
- take back = return
- take off = remove
- try on = test the fit or appearance of

PRACTICE

Read the story. There are five more errors. Find the errors and correct them. Rewrite your corrected sentences below.

Lois saw some suits on a sale rack. She looked over them. She picked out a black suit. She had a sweater on, so she took off it. She tried the jacket on. It fit perfectly. She took the skirt into the dressing room. She put on it. It fit, too. She took the jacket and skirt and hung up them. She walked to the cash register. She wrote a check. She made it out for $199.98. The clerk took the suit and folded up it. Lois picked the box up and left the store. She thought, "I can always take back it if I change my mind."

Corrected Sentences

1. <u>She looked them over.</u>
2. _____
3. _____
4. _____
5. _____
6. _____

MAKE IT WORK

Answer the question.

When you buy clothing, do you try it on first or do you buy it without trying it on?

_____

COULD YOU PUT OUT YOUR CIGAR?

Review: Separable Two-Word Verbs

Polite Requests

Could you	put out	your cigar?	
Could you	put	your cigar	out?
Could you	put	it	out?

Two-word verbs

call back	=	return a telephone call	
call up	=	telephone	
fill in	=	write information in spaces	
fill out	=	complete a form with information	
hand in	=	submit	
hand out	=	distribute	
hang up	=	place on a hanger	
hang up	=	end a telephone call	

pick up	=	come to get
pick out	=	select
put on	=	dress; put on one's body
put out	=	extinguish
take back	=	return
take off	=	remove

PRACTICE

Read each situation. Then respond by using a polite request and one of the two-word verbs above.

1. It is very cold outside. Your son is dressed in a T-shirt. Tell him to dress in a coat.

   Could you put on a coat? OR *Put your coat on.*

2. You are in the no-smoking section of a restaurant. A man is smoking a cigar. Tell him to extinguish his cigar.

   _____

3. You call a friend, and his answering machine answers the telephone. Leave a message on his machine. Say who you are. Then tell your friend to return your call tonight.

   _____

   _____

4. You and a friend are going to a restaurant, but you think it will be crowded. Ask your friend to telephone the restaurant and make a reservation.

   _____

COULD YOU PUT OUT YOUR CIGAR?

5. You work at a doctor's office. A new patient enters the office. Ask her to complete the medical form.

---

6. You work in an employment agency. A man looking for a job forgot to write his telephone number on his job application. Ask him to write this information in the space.

---

7. Your son left his jacket on the floor. Tell him to place it on a hanger.

---

8. You need to use a public telephone. It is an emergency. There is a woman using the phone. Ask her to end her telephone call.

---

9. You have just written a memo to all the employees at work. Ask your secretary to distribute the memo.

---

10. You are in a movie theater. You can't see the movie because the man in front of you has a hat on. Ask him to remove his hat.

---

11. A friend is going to the library. Ask your friend to return a book for you.

---

12. Your car doesn't work. Ask a co-worker to come to your house and take you to work tomorrow.

---

13. You are going to a wedding. You aren't sure what you should wear. Ask a friend to help you select something to wear.

---

14. An employee stole $50.00 from the company you work for. You are his boss. Ask the employee to submit his resignation today.

New Word: resignation = a formal letter of resigning or quitting one's job

I DON'T GET ALONG WITH HIM.

Separable and Inseparable Two- and Three-Word Verbs

Simple Past, Simple Present

> How's your cold?   I got over it.
>
> How's your job?   They laid me off.
>
> Note: Some two- and three-word verbs are not separable. This means that the object pronoun goes after the particle.
>
> irregular past tense verbs: lay → laid   run → ran
>
> **inseparable verbs**   **separable verbs**
>
> drop out of = stop attending   burn up = burn completely
>   a school or club   cut out = remove by cutting
> get over = recover from   give up = renounce; quit
> get along with = have a good   lay off = dismiss because of
>   relationship with   lack of work
> run into = collide with; hit   put away = return something to
> run out of = finish a supply   its proper place
>   of something
> run over = pass over with a
>   moving vehicle
>
> Three-word verbs are often inseparable but not always. Two-word verbs ending in *about, across, against,* or *into* are usually inseparable.

PRACTICE

Put the words in parentheses in the correct order.

John: Hi, honey. I'm home. How's your cold?

Mary   I guess I _____*got over it*_____ . I feel fine. You're home early.
              (1. it / got over)

John: They _____ .
Mary: Why?   (2. me / laid off)

John: It's my boss. I _____ . I guess I'll need
                        (3. him / don't get along with)
         the classified section of the newspaper. Where is it?

Mary: Sorry. I _____ of today's newspaper.
                    (4. it / cut out)

John: Why is the newspaper in such bad shape?

Mary: It was on the driveway. I accidentally _____ .
                                                (5. it / ran over)

I DON'T GET ALONG WITH HIM.

John: By the way, what happened to the garage door?

Mary: I _____ . It was an accident.
              (6. it / ran into)

John: I think I need some beer. Where is it?

Mary: We _____ last night. Remember?
              (7. it / ran out of)

John: And my cigarettes? Where are they?

Mary: I _____ .
              (8. them / threw away)

John: Why?

Mary: You shouldn't smoke. You should _____ . You know
                                      (9. it / give up)
    it's bad for your health.

John: Maybe I'll have some coffee. Where's the new coffee maker we
    bought?

Mary: It was broken, so I _____ to the store.
                     (10. it / took back)

John: Where are my slippers? They were here last night.

Mary: I _____ . They're in the closet.
              (11. them / put away)

John: I'm hungry. What's for dinner?

Mary: Nothing. I _____ .
                (12. it / burned up)

John: So let's go out for dinner.

Mary: I thought you had your Sierra Club meeting tonight.

John: No. I _____ . Let's go. Where's my jacket?
             (13. it / dropped out of)

Mary: I _____ .
             (14. it / hung up)

New Words: shape = condition

        classified section = pages in a newspaper that contain
                                advertisements for jobs and items
                                for sale

I MAKE SURE OF IT BEFORE I HAND MY PAPER IN.

Separable and Inseparable Two- and Three-Word Verbs

Simple Present

Do you look forward to your homework assignments, or do you dislike doing them?

I look forward to them.

inseparable verbs	**separable verbs**
come across = find unexpectedly	leave out = omit
look forward to = expect with pleasure	put off = postpone
make sure of = verify; become certain of	

 PRACTICE

Answer the questions. Use pronouns in your answers whenever possible.

1. Do you look forward to your homework assignments, or do you dislike doing them?

   I look forward to them.

2. Do you put off your homework assignments, or do you do them right away?

   _____

3. Do you usually leave out some answers, or do you fill them all in?

   _____

4. When you don't know the answer to a question, do you guess at it, or do you make sure of the answer before you hand in your paper?

   _____

5. When you can't spell a word, do you guess at the spelling, or do you look it up?

   _____

6. When you come across a new word, do you write it down, or do you try to remember it?

   _____

7. When you make a mistake on a homework assignment, do you erase it, or do you cross it out?

   _____

8. Do you turn in your homework assignments on time, or do you turn them in late?

   _____

I'M LOOKING FORWARD TO MY BIRTHDAY.

Review: Phrasal Verbs

Simple Present, Simple Past, Present Perfect

inseparable verb	I 'm looking forward to my birthday.
separable verb	After it's over, I 'll take all my gifts back to the store and get just what I want.

PRACTICE

Answer the questions. Use pronouns in your answers whenever possible.

1. When you write a letter, do you read it over before you mail it, or do you mail it without reading it?

   I read it over before I mail it.

2. Do you type up your letters, or do you write them by hand?

   _____

3. When you buy clothes, do you pick out bright colors or dark colors?

   _____

4. If you don't like something you bought at the store, do you take it back, or do you use it anyway?

   _____

5. Do you hang up your clothes when you take them off, or do you leave them on the floor?

   _____

6. Do you put things away after you use them, or do you leave them out?

   _____

7. Do you give back things you borrow, or do you keep them?

   _____

8. Do you put off your household chores, or do you do them right away?

   _____

9. What was the last thing you ran out of at home?

   _____

I'M LOOKING FORWARD TO MY BIRTHDAY.

10. What was the last thing you cut out of a newspaper?

    _____

11. What was the last thing you threw away?

    _____

12. How often do you call up your parents?

    _____

13. If you have a personal problem, who do you talk it over with?

    _____

14. If you're busy when a friend calls, how soon do you call him or her back?

    _____

15. If you don't know a phone number, where do you look it up?

    _____

16. How well do you get along with your co-workers?

    _____

17. Have you ever dropped out of school or a class? If so, when?

    _____

    _____

18. What celebration, party, or holiday are you looking forward to?

    _____

19. How long does it usually take you to get over a cold?

    _____

20. When was the last time you filled out a form? What kind of form was it?

    _____

    _____

New Word: by hand = done with the hands only, without a machine

APPENDIX

Two- and Three-Word Verbs (S = Separable)

burn up – burn completely (S)

call back – return a telephone call (S)

call up – telephone (S)

come across – find unexpectedly

cross out – draw a line through (S)

cut out – remove by cutting (S)

do over – do again (S)

drop out of – stop attending a school, a class, or a club

figure out – solve; find the answer to (S)

fill in – write information in spaces (S)

fill out – complete a form with information (S)

get along with – have a good relationship with

get over – recover from

give back – return (S)

give up – renounce; quit (S)
        resign; leave (S)

grow up – become an adult

hand in – submit (S)

hand out – distribute (S)

hang up – end a telephone call (S)
        place on a hanger (S)

lay down – set down; place (S)

lay off – dismiss because of lack of work (S)

leave out – omit (S)

look forward to – expect with pleasure

look over – examine; review (S)

look up – search for information (S)

make out – write (e.g., a check) (S)

make sure of – verify; become certain of

pick out – select (S)

pick up – lift; take in one's hand (S)
        go to get (S)

put away – return something to its proper place (S)

put off – postpone (S)

put on – dress; put on one's body (S)

put out – extinguish (S)
        display; put in view (S)

read over – read again (S)

run into – collide with; hit

run off – duplicate (S)

run out of – finish a supply of something

run over – pass over with a moving vehicle (S)

take back – return (S)

take off – remove (S)

talk over – discuss (S)

throw away – discard; get rid of (S)

try on – test the fit or appearance of something (S)

turn down – lower the power (S)

turn in – submit (S)

turn off – shut off the power of a machine or light (S)

turn on – start the power of a machine or light (S)

type up – type (S)

write down – write; record (S)

IRREGULAR VERBS

Simple Form	Past Form	Past Participle
be	was/were	been
become	became	become
begin	began	begun
break	broke	broken
bring	brought	brought
build	built	built
buy	bought	bought
catch	caught	caught
choose	chose	chosen
come	came	come
cut	cut	cut
do	did	done
drink	drank	drunk
drive	drove	driven
eat	ate	eaten
fall	fell	fallen
fight	fought	fought
find	found	found
fit	fit	fit
fly	flew	flown
forget	forgot	forgotten
get	got	gotten
give	gave	given
go	went	gone
grow	grew	grown
hang	hung	hung
have	had	had
hear	heard	heard
hide	hid	hidden
hit	hit	hit
hold	held	held
hurt	hurt	hurt
keep	kept	kept
know	knew	known
lay	laid	laid
leave	left	left
lose	lost	lost
make	made	made
meet	met	met

IRREGULAR VERBS

Simple Form	Past Form	Past Participle
put	put	put
quit	quit	quit
read	read	read
ride	rode	ridden
ring	rang	rung
run	ran	run
say	said	said
see	saw	seen
sell	sold	sold
send	sent	sent
set	set	set
shoot	shot	shot
sit	sat	sat
sleep	slept	slept
speak	spoke	spoken
spend	spent	spent
stand	stood	stood
steal	stole	stolen
swim	swam	swum
take	took	taken
tell	told	told
think	thought	thought
throw	threw	thrown
understand	understood	understood
wake	woke	woken
wear	wore	worn
win	won	won
write	wrote	written

UNCOUNTABLE NOUNS

architecture
art
baseball
bread
champagne
chemistry
clothing
coal
coffee
cooking
correspondence
crime
electricity
encouragement
engineering
entertainment
fishing
food
fun
furniture
gardening
gasoline
glass
golf
happiness
health
homework
housework
ice
ice cream
information

jewelry
love
luck
luggage
mail
money
music
oil
paint
perfume
photography
pollution
punch
sadness
soap
snow
spinach
stress
swimming
tea
tennis
time
transportation
trash
walking
water
weather
wine
work
yardwork

These nouns can be both countable and uncountable: crime, food, glass, time

ANSWERS TO EXERCISES

Page 1
2. lot
3. trees
4. story
5. stories
6. rooms
7. rooms
8. dishwasher
9. cabinets
10. bathrooms
11. bathroom
12. bathrooms

Page 2
2. —
3. —
4. biographies
5. —
6. —
7. dictionaries
8. —
9. —
10. —
11. games
12. —
13. —
14. hobbies
15. —
16. —
17. mysteries
18. pets
19. —
20. —

Page 3
Individual answers. Some possible answers are:
3. more (less)
4. more
5. fewer
6. more
7. less
8. fewer
9. more
10. less
11. more
12. less
13. more
14. fewer

Pages 4 and 5
3. the fewest
4. the most
5. the fewest
6. fewer
7. the most
8. the fewest
9. more
10. fewer
11. less
12. the least
13. less
14. the most
15. the most

Pages 6 and 7
2. report
3. hours
4. walking
5. swimming
6. Gardening
7. Miners
8. police officers
9. money
10. work
11. Librarians
12. stress
13. Coffee
14. gallons
15. ice cream
16. pounds
17. hamburgers
18. hamburger
19. dollars
20. cats
21. dogs
22. clothing
23. Blue jeans
24. students

Page 8
3. a
4. a
5. an
6. an
7. a
8. an
9. an
10. a
11. an
12. a
13. an
14. a
15. a
16. a
17. an
18. an
19. a
20. an
21. an
22. an
23. a
24. an
25. a

Page 9
Individual answers. Some possible answers are:
2. an ice cube
3. furniture
4. a floor
5. a shirt
6. a coat
7. a tie
8. a bow
9. pizza
10. bread (toast)
11. a newspaper
12. mail
13. a grape
14. a cherry
15. gasoline
16. paint

Page 10
2. a, a
3. a, a
4. the, the
5. a, a
6. the
7. the, the
8. the, the
9. the, the, the
10. the
11. the
12. the, the

Make It Work
Individual answers. Some possible answers are:
I keep it in the closet (under the bed).
I keep it on a hook in the closet.

Pages 11 and 12
2. —
3. The
4. a
5. —
6. —
7. an
8. The
9. —, —, —, —, —
10. a, —
11. The, the
12. —
13. —
14. a
15. The
16. —
17. The
18. a
19. a
20. the

135

Page 13

2. —, the
3. —, the
4. the, the
5. —
6. the, —
7. the, —
8. the
9. —, —
10. the

Pages 14 and 15

2. —, —
3. the, —
4. the, the
5. —, the
6. —
7. —, —, the, the, —
8. the, the
9. —, the
10. —, —, the
11. —
12. —

Page 16

2. The Atlantic is an ocean.
3. The Amazon is a river.
4. South America is a continent.
5. The Golden Gate is a bridge.
6. Hawaii is an island.
7. Fuji is a mountain.
8. The Hilton is a hotel.
9. Harvard is a university.
10. Broadway is a street.
11. Waikiki is a beach.
12. The Louvre is a museum.

Page 17

2. a	14. a
3. —	15. The
4. The	16. a
5. a	17. —
6. The	18. the
7. —	19. the
8. the	20. —
9. a	21. the
10. the	22. a
11. the	23. —
12. —	24. The
13. the	25. the

Pages 18 and 19

2. He has a personal fortune of $500 million.
3. He lives on a farm in Sussex, England.
4. He owns (has) a farm in Scotland.
5. earns (makes) $15 million a year.
6. She owns (has) houses in New York, Hollywood, Hawaii, and Nashville.
7. She owns several restaurants.
8. She owns (has) a $6 million amusement park called Dollywood.
9. has a personal fortune of $200 million.
10. He lives in (has, owns) a house in Encino, California, with 50 rooms.
11. He owns (has) a private zoo.
12. earns (makes) $10 million a year.
13. She has (owns) houses in Nashville and Aspen.
14. She has (owns) a yacht and a helicopter.
15. She owns (has) a health club and a museum in Nashville.
16. He earns (makes) $35 million a year.
17. He lives in (has, owns) a mansion built by King Henry VIII in England.
18. He has (owns) an art collection worth $15 million.
19. He has (owns) a collection of sunglasses worth $500,000.
20. He drives (owns, has) a Rolls-Royce, a Bently, and a Ferrari.

Pages 20 and 21

2. grew
3. went
4. read
5. had
6. said
7. spent
8. was
9. decided
10. wanted
11. wrote
12. rejected
13. published
14. was
15. thought
16. said
17. came
18. wrote
19. became
20. confessed

Page 22

Individual answers.

Page 23

2. grew
3. go
4. tutored
5. read
6. make
7. challenged
8. accept
9. completed
10. publish
11. rejected
12. had
13. have
14. thought
15. think

Pages 24 and 25

The first day of the trip, he sat opposite a Frenchman for lunch. The Frenchman arrived late. As he came in, he turned to Mr. Jones and said, "Bon appetit." Mr. Jones, who knew no French at all, thought that the Frenchman was giving his name, so he stood up and said, "Jones."

The second day the Frenchman arrived late and said, "Bon appetit." Mr. Jones got up and said, "Jones." The third day the same thing happened.

The fourth day, as Mr. Jones was taking a morning walk around the boat, he met an old friend. His friend asked him how the trip was going. Mr. Jones mentioned that there was an Italian man named

Bonappetit opposite him at lunch. His friend understood the situation immediately. He explained that the man wasn't Italian. He told Mr. Jones that the man was French and that he was wishing him a pleasant lunch. Mr. Jones decided to correct the situation.

Mr. Jones arrived late for lunch that day. When he walked into the dining area, the Frenchman was already eating. Mr. Jones said, "Bon appetit." The Frenchman smiled and said, "Jones."

Page 26

Individual answers. Some possible answers are:
I'll quit smoking (I'll exercise more, stop wasting time, work harder, be nicer to people, go to church more often, save some money, be on time, be more organized, spend more time with my family).
I won't worry so much (work so hard, eat so fast, watch so much TV, spend so much money).
I won't eat "junk" food (criticize people).

Page 27

Individual answers beginning with *I'll* and *I won't*.

Page 28

2. After he sees San Juan, he'll go to St. Thomas.
3. When he's in St. Thomas, he'll do some shopping.
4. After he spends a day in St. Thomas, he'll go to Martinique.
5. When he's in Martinique, he'll buy some French perfume.
6. When he's in Martinique, he'll also go swimming.
7. After he sees Martinique, he'll go to Barbados.
8. After he leaves Barbados, he'll go to La Guaira.

9. When he's in La Guaira, he'll visit Caracas.
10. After he visits Caracas, he'll go home.

Page 29

2. are	9. works
3. wore	10. works
4. carried	11. is
5. were	12. will attend
6. was	13. 'll (will) major
7. served	14. will live
8. graduated	

Page 30

2. He hid his lottery ticket under his mattress.
3. He has a job at a minimarket.
4. He lives with his mother and sister in a two-bedroom apartment.
5. He drives a 1988 Ford.
6. He earns $16,000 a year.
7. He'll help his family in the Philippines.
8. He'll buy a house.
9. He'll give some of his money to charity.
10. He won't buy a new car.

Pages 31–33

2. is shopping
3. have
4. 'm taking
5. have
6. 'm learning
7. think
8. is
9. has
10. seems
11. feel
12. is growing
13. 's majoring
14. costs
15. likes
16. dislikes
17. wants
18. remember
19. own
20. see

21. belong
22. is getting

Make It Work

Individual answers. Some possible answers are:
I like the class (the teacher, the students in the class).
I think I'm learning a lot.
My English is getting better.
I have a good teacher. I think the class is too expensive. I don't like the hours of the class.

Page 34

3. He's stopping in Antigua on December 3rd.
4. He stops in Antigua on December 3rd.
5. He's visiting Martinique on December 5th.
6. He visits Martinique on December 5th.
7. He's going to Trinidad on December 8th.
8. He goes to Trinidad on December 8th.
9. He's staying in Caracas on December 9th and 10th.
10. He stays in Caracas on December 9th and 10th.
11. He's flying back to Puerto Rico on December 11th.
12. He flies back to Puerto Rico on December 11th.

Page 35

2. was depositing
3. were standing
4. were talking
5. was writing
6. was endorsing
7. were filling
8. was sitting
9. were applying
10. were waiting

Page 36

2. was taking, rang
3. were having, arrived
4. rang, was talking
5. was talking, started

6. was feeding, had
7. were playing, started
8. was eating, began
9. was sleeping, decided
10. was watching, came

Page 37

2. She's been watering the lawn for four hours.
3. They've been pulling weeds for an hour.
4. She's been planting flowers for two hours.
5. They've been painting the house for six hours.
6. He's been putting up the storm windows for two hours.
7. They've been washing the windows for four hours.
8. He's been fixing the driveway for three hours.
9. She's been sweeping the patio for an hour.
10. He's been trimming the bushes for three hours.

Page 38

2. He'll be working in the sales department.
3. He'll be hiring salespeople.
4. He'll be developing a sales team.
5. He'll be managing the sales team.
6. He'll be reporting to the president of the company.
7. He'll be traveling ten days a month.
8. He'll be going to conferences.
9. He'll be giving speeches.
10. He'll be writing sales reports.

Page 39

3. They're working on the report.
4. they'll be working on the report.
5. she'll be sitting at the switchboard.
6. She's sitting at the switchboard.
7. he'll be waiting for the report.

8. he was waiting for the report.
9. they'll be eating lunch.
10. they were eating lunch.

Page 40

2. I haven't seen the new language lab yet.
3. I've already chosen an English class.
4. I haven't seen the foreign student advisor yet.
5. I've already read the student handbook.
6. I haven't met the instructor yet.
7. I haven't spoken to the instructor yet.
8. I've already been (gone) to the bookstore.
9. I haven't bought a dictionary yet.
10. I've already done the homework.

Page 41

Individual answers.

Page 42

2. Have you ever spent Egyptian money?
3. Have you ever gone to a bazaar?
4. Have you ever bought Egyptian jewelry?
5. Have you ever taken a boat trip up the Nile?
6. Have you ever ridden a camel?
7. Have you ever stood in front of a temple?
8. Have you ever seen the pyramids?
9. Have you ever read a book on the history of Egypt?
10. Have you ever gotten up at 4:30 to see a sunrise?
11. Have you ever worn a veil?
12. Have you ever brought home souvenirs of your trip?

Page 43

Individual answers.

Page 44

2. The guests had arrived.
3. Everyone had had a glass of champagne.
4. The bride and groom had cut the cake.
5. Everyone had eaten a piece of cake.
6. The band had started to play.
7. The bride had danced with the groom.
8. The bride had thrown the bouquet.
9. Several people had left the reception.
10. The bride and groom had left the reception.

Page 45

2. They hadn't eaten out in a long time.
3. He hadn't cleaned out the garage in a long time.
4. I hadn't seen a good movie in a long time.
5. We hadn't been to the beach in a long time.
6. They hadn't taken a vacation in a long time.
7. I hadn't read a good book in a long time.
8. We hadn't played miniature golf in a long time.
9. They hadn't visited their family in a long time.
10. I hadn't been to the doctor in a long time.

Pages 46 and 47

2. She'd already met with the Art Department.
3. She'd (She had) already gotten a report from the sales department.
4. She'd (She had) already written the Avco report.
5. She'd (She had) already typed the Avco report.
6. She'd (She had) already copied the Avco report.

7. She'd (She had) already put the Avco report on Mr. Ripley's desk.
8. She'd (She had) already (eaten) lunch.
9. She hadn't sent a fax to Avco yet.
10. She hadn't opened the mail yet.
11. She hadn't filed the correspondence from yesterday yet.
12. She hadn't given Mr. Ripley his telephone messages yet.
13. She hadn't met with Mr. Ripley yet.

Page 48

2. Until last week, he'd (he had) never flown over the Atlantic Ocean.
3. Until last week, he'd (he had) never seen snow.
4. Until last week, he'd (he had) never spoken English.
5. Until last week, he'd (he had) never met an American.
6. Until last week, he'd (he had) never eaten a hamburger.
7. Until last week, he'd (he had) never drunk a milkshake.
8. Until last week, he'd (he had) never heard country music.
9. Until last week, he'd (he had) never watched an American TV program.
10. Until last week, he'd (he had) never gone (been) to a barbecue.

Page 49

2. She'll have bought the food.
3. She'll have ironed the tablecloth.
4. She'll have set the table.
5. She'll have decorated the living room.
6. She'll have cooked the meal.
7. She'll have made the punch.
8. She'll have baked a cake.
9. She'll have changed into a party dress.

10. She'll have turned on the CD player.

Pages 50 and 51

2. By July 1st, she'd (she had) driven 4,500 miles.
   As of today, she's (she has) driven 6,000 miles.
   By January 1st, she'll (she will) have driven 11,000 miles.
3. By July 1st, she'd (she had) spent $7,000.
   As of today, she's (she has) spent $11,000.
   By January 1st, she'll (she will) have spent $14,500.
4. By July 1st she'd (she had) visited several friends.
   As of today, she's (she has) visited a dozen friends.
   By January 1st, she'll (she will) have visited a lot of friends.
5. By July 1st, she hadn't bought any souvenirs. (By July 1st, she'd bought no souvenirs.)
   As of today, she's (she has) bought a few souvenirs.
   By January 1st, she'll (she will) have bought a lot of souvenirs.
6. By July 1st, she hadn't seen the Pacific Ocean.
   As of today, she's (she has) seen the Pacific Ocean.
   By January 1st, she'll (she will) have seen the Pacific (Ocean) twice.
7. By July 1st, she'd (she had) gone to Niagara Falls.
   As of today, she's (she has) gone to Niagara Falls and Disneyland.
   By January 1st, she'll (she will) have gone to Niagara Falls, Disneyland, and the Grand Canyon.
8. By July 1st, she'd (she had) written 90 postcards.
   As of today, she's (she has) written 135 postcards.

By January 1st, she'll (she will) have written 180 postcards.

Page 52

2. traveled
3. 've been
4. spent
5. flew
6. went
7. hired
8. saw
9. went
10. drove
11. visited
12. haven't been
13. have never traveled
14. 've never heard
15. has been

Page 53

2. broke
3. woke
4. called
5. had left
6. searched
7. had stolen
8. had forgotten
9. questioned
10. 'd (had) seen
11. were
12. saw

Page 54

2. I hope (that) you pass the examination.
3. I hope (that) they get married.
4. I hope (that) she gets a promotion.
5. I hope (that) he wins the election.
6. I hope (that) they get engaged.
7. I hope (that) he receives an award.
8. I hope (that) you get a raise.
9. I hope (that) he graduates from law school.
10. I hope (that) she's (she is) accepted to medical school.

2. I wish (that) I didn't have to worry about money.
3. I wish (that) I didn't have to buy clothes.
4. I wish (that) I had a beautiful fur coat.
5. I wish (that) I lived in a big house.
6. I wish (that) I were independent.
7. I wish (that) I didn't have to work.
8. I wish (that) I could sleep until noon every day.
9. I wish (that) I didn't have to be anywhere at any particular time.
10. I wish (that) I were a cat.

Page 56

Possible answers are given.

3. He wishes (that) he knew some Americans.
4. He hopes (that) he can meet (will get to know) some Americans soon.
5. He wishes (that) he had (could get) a part-time job.
6. He hopes (that) he can get (find) a part-time job soon.
7. He wishes (that) he had (could buy) a car.
8. He hopes (that) he can buy a car soon.
9. He wishes (that) he lived near (closer to) the university.
10. He hopes (that) he can (will) find a room (an apartment) closer to the university.
11. He wishes (that) he had more money.
12. He hopes (that) he has (will have) more money soon. (He hopes he can earn some money soon.)

Make It Work

Individual answers. Some possible answers are:

I wish I could speak English more clearly.

I hope I can speak more clearly after this class.

Page 57

2. If you open a new account at United Bank, you'll receive a free TV.
3. If you buy two cans of King Tuna, you'll save 60¢.
4. If you visit our pharmacy, you'll get $2.00 off on any prescription.
5. If you call this number now, you'll get a clock radio.
6. If you visit our shop, you'll receive a free gift.
7. If you purchase one chicken dinner, you'll get the second one free.
8. If you purchase (buy) a Kobe TV now, you'll get 40% off.
9. If you attend our grand opening, you'll receive a free plant.
10. If you buy an airline ticket by May 1st, you'll get 50% off.

Make It Work

If you buy (purchase) a 30-ounce can of Colombian coffee (at Big Time Supermarket), you'll get (receive) 30¢ off.

Page 58

Individual answers beginning with *If I owned* or *had*.

Page 59

Individual answers beginning with *I'd* or *I wouldn't*.

Pages 60 and 61

2. If I'd (I had) been Thomas Becket, I'd (I would) have (I wouldn't have) died for my church.
3. If I'd (I had) been Susan B. Anthony, I'd (I would) have (I wouldn't have) fought for women's rights.
4. If I'd (I had) been Grace Kelly, I wouldn't have (I'd have) had given up my movie career to marry a prince.

5. If I'd (I had) been Jean-Paul Sartre, I wouldn't have (I'd have) refused the Nobel Prize.
6. If I'd (I had) been King Edward of England, I wouldn't have (I'd have) given up my throne for a woman.
7. If I'd (I had) been Joan of Arc, I'd (I would) have (I wouldn't have) died for my country.
8. If I'd (I had) been Martin Luther King, I'd (I would) have (I wouldn't have) fought for civil rights.
9. If I'd (I had) been Charlie Chaplin, I wouldn't have (I'd have) given up my U. S. citizenship.
10. If I'd (I had) been Cleopatra, I wouldn't have killed myself.
11. If I'd (I had) been Napoleon, I wouldn't have (I'd have) fought the Battle of Waterloo.
12. If I'd (I had) been Mahatma Gandhi, I'd (I would) have (I wouldn't have) fasted for my political beliefs.
13. If I'd (I had) been Jane Addams, I'd (I would) have (I wouldn't have) improved working conditions for the poor.
14. If I'd (I had) been Queen Elizabeth I, I'd (I would) have (I wouldn't have) gotten married.
15. If I'd (I had) been Abraham Lincoln, I'd (I would) (I wouldn't) have freed the slaves.

Page 62

2. If she hadn't been in a hurry, she wouldn't have had to run to the train station.
3. If she hadn't had to run to the train station, she wouldn't have slipped on the ice.

4. If she hadn't slipped on the ice, her briefcase wouldn't have opened.
5. If her briefcase hadn't opened, her papers wouldn't have been scattered everywhere.
6. If her papers hadn't been scattered everywhere, she wouldn't have had to pick them up.
7. If she hadn't had to pick them up, she wouldn't have arrived at the train station late.
8. If she hadn't arrived at the train station late, she wouldn't have missed her train.
9. If she hadn't missed her train, she wouldn't have arrived at the office late.
10. If she hadn't arrived at the office late, her boss wouldn't have been angry.

Page 63
2. She wishes she'd (she had) been ready.
3. She wishes she'd (she had) had time to set the table in advance.
4. She wishes she hadn't forgotten to serve the appetizer.
5. She wishes the roast had been done on time.
6. She wishes she hadn't burned the potatoes.
7. She wishes she hadn't spilled wine all over the tablecloth.
8. She wishes the dessert had turned out.
9. She wishes she'd (she had) been able to spend time with her guests.
10. She wishes the evening hadn't been a disaster.

Page 64
Individual answers beginning with *I'll, I'd,* or *I'd have:*
2. I'll... .
3. I'd... .

4. I'd (I wouldn't) have... .
5. I'll... .
6. I'd (I wouldn't) have... .
7. I'd (I wouldn't)... .
8. I'd (I wouldn't)... .
9. I'd (I wouldn't) have... .
10. I'll... .

Page 65
Individual answers.

Page 66
Answers may vary.
2. I should do the laundry, but I'd rather go to the movies.
3. I should clean the house, but I'd rather watch the baseball game.
4. I should mow the lawn, but I'd rather take a nap.
5. I should fix dinner, but I'd rather go out.
6. I should get up early, but I'd rather stay in bed.
7. I should drink a glass of water, but I'd rather have some soda.
8. I should do the dishes, but I'd rather watch television.
9. I should go to work, but I'd rather stay home.
10. I should do my work, but I'd rather go to a party.

Page 67
2. have to
3. don't have to
4. have to (must)
5. must not
6. have to (must)
7. must not
8. don't have to
9. must not
10. don't have to

Page 68
Individual answers.
Make It Work
Some possible answers are:
He could read.
He could play cards with a friend.

Page 69
Individual answers. Some possible answers are:
3. It could be a hat.
4. It might be a hill.
5. It could be an M.
6. It might be two mountains.
7. It could be a mustache.
8. It might be two birds.
9. It could be a fried egg.
10. It might be a cup and saucer.

Page 70
2. She shouldn't have married Tom.
3. She should have married Rolly Green.
4. They should have invested their money wisely.
5. He should have saved more money.
6. She shouldn't have quit her job.
7. They shouldn't have sold their piano.
8. She should have learned to drive.
9. She shouldn't have cut her hair.
10. They shouldn't have bought such an expensive house.

Page 71
2. She could have fallen off the ladder.
3. He could have caught a cold.
4. You could have hurt your back.
5. She could have had an accident.
6. He could have been hit by a car.
7. They (The children) could have shot someone.
8. They could have gotten hurt.
9. She could have gotten a shock.
10. He (The little boy) could have drowned.

Page 72

2. She used to live with her parents.
3. She used to play with dolls.
4. She used to wear cowboy hats and blue jeans (blue jeans).
5. She used to dress up in her mother's clothes.
6. She used to climb trees.
7. She used to play baseball in the street.
8. She used to collect stamps.
9. She used to take ballet lessons.
10. She used to read comic books.

Page 73

2. You didn't use to drink coffee.
3. You didn't use to smoke a lot.
4. You didn't use to like to be alone.
5. You didn't use to read a lot.
6. You didn't use to wear glasses.
7. You didn't use to enjoy classical music.
8. You didn't use to like concerts.
9. You didn't use to like modern art.
10. You didn't use to enjoy serious discussions.
11. You didn't use to like foreign films.
12. You didn't use to like to study.

Page 74

2. He isn't use to working
3. He isn't use to commuting
4. He isn't use to living
5. He isn't use to living
6. He isn't use to cooking
7. He isn't use to cleaning
8. He isn't use to doing
9. He isn't use to supporting
10. He isn't use to paying

Make It Work

I'm used to (I'm not use to)
I'm used to (I'm not use to)

Page 75

2. be
3. laid
4. be
5. remember
6. left
7. look
8. looked
9. taken
10. help
11. get
12. stay
13. make
14. find

Pages 76 and 77

Individual answers. Some possible answers are:

2. You should quit smoking. (You shouldn't smoke.)
3. You should have made reservations. (You should have gone somewhere else.)
4. You should go to France (Germany, Italy).
5. You should have studied (for your Spanish test).
6. You could rent a video. (You could watch a movie on TV.)
7. You shouldn't go to the party. (You should study before you go to the party.)
8. You should have arrived earlier (called, telephoned). (You shouldn't have been so late.)
9. You should wear a raincoat (rain boots). (You should take an umbrella.)
10. You could have asked a friend to drive you home. (You could have taken a bus, a taxi.)
11. You should learn some Spanish before you go (to Mexico).
12. You could fix an omelette (scrambled eggs).

Page 78

Individual answers.

Page 79

2. They're being typed.
3. It's being made.
4. It's being opened.
5. It's being printed.
6. They're being added.
7. They're being delivered.
8. It's being copied.
9. They're being signed.
10. They're being sent.
11. It's being used.
12. It's being written.

Make It Work

(The check) is being signed.

Page 80

2. wasn't built
3. was built
4. wasn't designed
5. was copied
6. wasn't used
7. was designed
8. wasn't painted
9. was removed
10. wasn't made
11. was made
12. was bought
13. were replaced
14. was remodeled
15. were replaced

Page 81

2. The meeting will be held at the Manor Hotel.
3. All salespeople will be expected to attend.
4. Transportation will be provided.
5. Sales will be discussed from 9:00 to 11:00.
6. A sales report will be given from 11:00 to 12:00.
7. Lunch will be served from 12:00 to 1:00.
8. The people will be divided into two groups from 2:00 to 4:00.
9. A cocktail party will be given at 5:00.
10. Dinner will be served at 8:00.

Make It Work

An important meeting will be
held tomorrow at 3:00 in the
conference room. All employees
are expected to attend.

Page 82

2. saw
3. called
4. arrived
5. was rushed
6. examined
7. was taken
8. wasn't (was not) injured
9. was bruised
10. wasn't (was not) broken
11. told
12. was notified

Page 83

Individual answers.

Page 84

Individual answers ending in:

2. ...funnier.
3. ...more educational.
4. ...more amusing.
5. ...sillier.
6. ...more informative.
7. ...more interesting.
8. ...more terrifying.
9. ...more exciting.
10. ...more popular.

Pages 85 and 86

2. the largest
3. the mightiest
4. (the) most exotic
5. the most exciting
6. the biggest
7. the bravest
8. the tallest
9. (the) most spectacular
10. the prettiest
11. the most fantastic
12. the most delicious
13. the best
14. The most wonderful
15. the most expensive

Page 87

2. No. He should have hit the
   ball harder.
3. No. He should have hit the
   ball harder.
4. No. He should have gone to
   the net more quickly.
5. No. He should have run
   faster.
6. No. He should have served
   more accurately.
7. No. He should have played
   more skillfully.
8. No. He should have gone to
   the net more frequently.
9. No. He should have
   concentrated harder.
10. No. He should have played
    better.

Page 88

2. any
3. any
4. no
5. none
6. any
7. any
8. none
9. any
10. None
11. any
12. no

Make It Work

I have some change. (I don't have
any change.)
I have some (no) gum. (I don't
have any gum.)
I have some (no) tissues. (I don't
have any tissues.)

Page 89

There was no (wasn't any) mail
today.
What? You mean there was no
(wasn't any) mail delivery?
No. I mean there was no (wasn't
any) mail for you today.
I never get anything (I don't ever
get anything) in the mail.
That's because you never (don't
ever) write to anyone.
That's not true. It's because no one
ever writes to me.

Page 90

2. I can't dance very well.
3. I always thought I danced
   badly.

4. I feel terrible today.
5. You don't look bad.
6. In fact, you look good.
7. They fit perfectly.

Make It Work

Some possible answers are:
Your new suit is beautiful.
That suit looks good on you.

Pages 91 and 92

2. Air pollution comes from
   incinerators and smokestacks.
3. It also comes from
   automobiles, buses, and
   trucks.
4. Water pollution comes from
   chemical waste and trash.
5. People throw trash into our
   rivers, lakes, and oceans.
6. Factories dump chemical
   waste, oil, and detergents
   into our water.
7. Noise pollution comes from
   cars, car horns, and
   subways.
8. Construction work and loud
   radios can cause noise
   pollution.
9. Our world is becoming
   unhealthy for people and
   animals.
10. However, people, companies,
    and the government can do
    something about it.

Pages 93 and 94

2. He can't take shorthand,
   and he doesn't have any
   experience.
3. He didn't make a good
   impression in the interview,
   so Mr. Simon isn't going to
   hire him.
4. Kim can type, but she can't
   use a computer.
5. She was pleasant and polite
   in the interview, but Mr.
   Simon isn't going to hire her.
6. She can't take shorthand,
   and she doesn't have any
   experience.

7. Mary can type, and she can use a computer.
8. She can take shorthand, but she doesn't have any experience.
9. She didn't make a good impression in the interview, so Mr. Simon isn't going to hire her.
10. Carlos can take shorthand, and he can type.
11. He can use a computer, but he can't use a fax machine.
12. He was pleasant and polite in the interview, and he has a lot of experience.
13. Carlos is the best person for the job, so Mr. Simon is going to offer the job to Carlos.

Page 95

2. Although Ruby hasn't been with the company for very long, she deserves a promotion.
3. Because Ruby works hard, she deserves a promotion.
4. Because Irma doesn't work hard, she doesn't deserve a promotion.
5. Although Irma always gets to work on time, she doesn't finish her work.
6. Although Ruby is sometimes late to work, she always finishes her work.
7. Because Irma doesn't always finish her work, she doesn't deserve a promotion.
8. Because Ruby is the best employee, she's going to get a promotion.

Page 96
Individual answers.

Page 97
Individual answers.

Page 98
Individual answers.

Page 99

2. says (that) she will get married and be happy.
3. says (that) someone has a pleasant surprise for him.
4. says (that) I will receive a lot of money.
5. says (that) he will change his employment soon.
6. says (that) she will receive something new this week.
7. says (that) an old friend will bring me good news.
8. says (that) an unexpected event will bring him money.
9. says (that) I will have many pleasures ahead.
10. says (that) he will take a long trip soon.

Make It Work

It says (that) I can expect a change in residence soon.

Pages 100 and 101

2. told		9. said	
3. said		10. told	
4. told		11. told	
5. told		12. told	
6. told		13. said	
7. said		14. told	
8. told		15. told	

Make It Work

Elvira Mendoza told a lie. She told the police that she was at the hairdresser's, but the hairdresser said (that) she didn't show up.

Page 102

2. The doctor told Mrs. Murphy not to drink any alcohol.
3. The doctor told her to get lots of rest.
4. The doctor told her to go to bed early at night.
5. The doctor told her not to go back to work for a week.
6. The doctor told her not to smoke any cigarettes.
7. The doctor told her not to eat rich food.
8. The doctor told her to come in for a checkup next week.
9. The doctor told her to take one spoonful of medicine twice a day.
10. The doctor told her not to worry.

Page 103

2. She told him not to talk with his mouth full.
3. She told him to eat everything on his plate.
4. She told him not to eat between meals.
5. She told him to stand up straight.
6. She told him not to put his feet on the furniture.
7. She told him to be polite to adults.
8. She told him to put his toys away.
9. She told him not to cross the street alone.
10. She told him not to talk to strangers.

Pages 104 and 105

2. she couldn't get married until she was 18.
3. her boyfriend wasn't good enough for her.
4. she was making a big mistake.
5. she was being very foolish.
6. she'd (she would) be sorry later.
7. she hadn't known him long enough.
8. her boyfriend wouldn't be able to support her.
9. she couldn't get married without her parents' consent.
10. she needed her parents' consent.

Page 106

2. he wouldn't be in today.
3. she'd (she would) be late this morning.
4. she'd (she would) be in at 10:30.
5. he needed the report right away.
6. it was urgent.
7. the report wouldn't be ready until tomorrow.
8. she was very busy today.
9. he couldn't come to the meeting today.
10. he'd (he would) call back later.

Page 107

2. The interviewer asked Diane if she could use a computer.
3. He asked Diane if she had any office experience.
4. He asked Diane if she would work overtime.
5. He asked her if she was a high school graduate.
6. He asked her if she'd (she would) work at night.
7. The interviewer asked her if she could take shorthand.
8. He asked if she had any references.
9. The interviewer asked if she'd (she would) work on Saturdays.
10. The interviewer asked Diane if she could begin tomorrow.

Page 108

2. He asked Diane how many languages she could speak.
3. The interviewer asked Diane how fast she could type.
4. He asked Diane what high school she had graduated from. (He asked Diane what high school she graduated from.)
5. He asked her when she had graduated from high school. (He asked her when she graduated from high school.)

6. He asked her how much office experience she had had. (He asked her how much office experience she had.)
7. He asked her how long she had worked for Selby Company. (He asked her how long she worked for Selby Company.)
8. He asked Diane how fast she could take shorthand.
9. He asked Diane why she wanted to work for A.B.C. Company.
10. He asked her when she could begin work.

Page 109

2. I can't believe he asked her if she was happily married.
3. I can't believe he asked her if she had any children.
4. I can't believe he asked her why she didn't have any children.
5. I can't believe he asked her if she was planning on having a family.
6. I can't believe he asked her how much money her husband made.
7. I can't believe he asked her how old she was.
8. I can't believe he asked her what religion she was.
9. I can't believe he asked her what political party she belonged to.
10. I can't believe he asked her if she had any personal problems.

Page 110

2. anyone
3. no one
4. nothing
5. nothing
6. someone
7. someone
8. anyone

9. something
10. anything

Page 111

2. Who's
3. Who's
4. whose
5. Whose
6. Whose
7. Whose
8. Who's
9. who's
10. Whose
11. Who's
12. Who's

Page 112

2. They're
3. They're
4. Their
5. there
6. their
7. There
8. their
9. their
10. There
11. their
12. there
13. their
14. they're

Page 113

2. to
3. on
4. in
5. onto
6. into
7. out of
8. off
9. away from

Make It Work

Some possible answers are:
There was a bird cage on the table. (A bird cage was on the table.) There was a bird in the bird cage. (A bird was in the bird cage.) A (The) cat jumped onto the table. He knocked the bird cage off the table. He put his paw into the bird cage. He pulled the bird out of the bird cage and ate it.

Pages 114 and 115
2. in, on
3. at, in
4. at
5. On, on
6. from, to
7. in
8. from, to
9. On
10. in
11. In, on
12. At
13. at, from, to
14. in
15. On, from, to

Page 116
2. since   9. for
3. For   10. For
4. ago   11. ago
5. for   12. for
6. ago   13. ago
7. since   14. since
8. since   15. for

Page 117
2. at   8. for
3. to   9. at
4. to   10. to
5. about   11. at
6. for   12. about
7. about

Page 118
2. at, at   7. about
3. of (about)   8. in (with)
4. about   9. of
5. at   10. about, at
6. of

Page 119
2. At   10. about
3. about   11. to
4. in   12. at
5. On   13. about
6. in   14. in
7. at   15. of
8. at   16. to
9. In   17. about

Page 120
2. finding
3. start
4. move
5. rent
6. spending
7. obtaining
8. work
9. see
10. hearing

Page 121
2. look it up
3. cross it out
4. figure it out
5. talk it over
6. read it over
7. hand it in
8. throw them away

Page 122
2. Do you want me to fill it in today?
3. Do you want me to look it up today?
4. Do you want me to add them up today?
5. Do you want me to write it down today?
6. Do you want me to type it up today?
7. Do you want me to run them off today?
8. Do you want me to hand them out to all the salespeople today?
9. Do you want me to call him up today?
10. Do you want me to turn it in to Mr. Suzuki today?

Make It Work
Do you want me to do it over?

Page 123
2. She had a sweater on, so she took it off.
3. She put it on. (She put the skirt on. She put on the skirt.)
4. She took the jacket and skirt and hung them up.
5. The clerk took the suit and folded it up.

6. She thought, "I can always take it back if I change my mind." ("I can always take the suit back if I change my mind." "I can always take back the suit if I change my mind.")

Pages 124 and 125
2. Could you please put your cigar out? (Could you please put out your cigar?)
3. This is (your name). Could you (please) call me back tonight?
4. Could you call the restaurant up and make a reservation? (Could you call up the restaurant and make a reservation?)
5. Could you (please) fill the (medical) form out? (Could you fill out the medical form?)
6. Could you (please) fill your telephone number in (on your job application?) (Could you fill in your telephone number?)
7. Could you hang your jacket up? (Hang up your jacket.)
8. (This is an emergency.) Could you (please) hang the telephone up? (Could you hang up the telephone?)
9. Could you (please) hand the memo out (to all the employees)? (Could you hand out the memo?)
10. (I can't see the movie.) Could you (please) take your hat off? (Could you take off your hat?)
11. Could you (please) take a book back for me? (Could you take back this book for me?)
12. (My car doesn't work.) Could you (please) pick me up (and take me to work) tomorrow?
13. Could you (please) help me pick out something to wear (to the wedding)?

14. Please hand in your resignation today. (Please hand your resignation in today.

Pages 126 and 127
2. laid me off
3. don't get along with him
4. cut it out
5. ran over it
6. ran into it
7. ran out of it
8. threw them away
9. give it up
10. took it back
11. put them away
12. burned it up
13. dropped out of it
14. hung it up

Page 128
2. I put them off. OR I do them right away.
3. I leave some answers out. OR I fill them all in.
4. I guess at it. OR I make sure of it.
5. I guess at it. OR I look it up.
6. I write it down. OR I try to remember it.
7. I erase it. OR I cross it out.
8. I turn them in on time. OR I turn them in late.

Pages 129 and 130
Individual answers. Some possible answers are:
2. I type them up. OR I write them by hand.
3. I pick out bright colors. (I pick bright colors out.) OR I pick out dark colors. (I pick dark colors out.)
4. I take it back. OR I use it anyway.
5. I hang them up. OR I leave them on the floor.
6. I put them away. OR I leave them out.
7. I give them back. OR I keep them.

8. I put them off. OR I do them right away.
9. I ran out of tissues (soap, milk, cigarettes, etc.).
10. I cut out a coupon (an advertisement, a job listing).
11. I threw away an old grocery list (an empty milk carton).
12. I call them up once a week (twice a month). (I call up my parents every day.)
13. (If I have a personal problem,) I talk it over with my mother (my father, my older brother, my husband, my wife).
14. I call him or her back right away. OR I call him or her back the next day.
15. I look it up in the telephone book (directory).
16. I get along with them very well. OR I don't get along with them very well.
17. (Yes, I have.) I dropped out of (name of school or class) in (month or year). OR No, I haven't.
18. I'm looking forward to Christmas (my birthday, my graduation party, etc.).
19. It (usually) takes me three or four days (a week) to get over it.
20. I filled out a job application (an insurance form, a medical form) in (month or year, etc.).